INCLUSIVE
LEADERSHIP

NAVIGATING
ORGANISATIONAL
COMPLEXITY

SILE WALSH

Publisher/Distributor: ELIS Institute

ISBN Paperback: 9781738494507

ISBN e-books: 9781738494514

Email address: Books@silewalsh.com

Ordering Information:

Quantity sales. Special discounts are available on quantity purchases by corporations, associations, and others. For details, contact the publisher at the address above.

Disclaimer:

This publication is designed to provide accurate and authoritative information in regard to the subject matter covered. It is sold with the understanding that neither the author nor the publisher is engaged in rendering legal, investment, accounting or other professional services. While the publisher and author have used their best efforts in preparing this book, they make no representations or warranties with respect to the accuracy or completeness of the contents of this book and specifically disclaim any implied warranties of merchantability or fitness for a particular purpose. No warranty may be created or extended by sales representatives or written sales materials. The advice and strategies contained herein may not be suitable for your situation. You should consult with a professional when appropriate. Neither the publisher nor the author shall be liable for any loss of profit or any other commercial damages, including but not limited to special, incidental, consequential, personal, or other damages.

Author Sile walsh

Contributors Lynn Killick and Dr Liz Wilson

Book Cover by Daniel Eyenegho

1st edition 2024

INCLUSIVE
LEADERSHIP

About the Author

Sile Walsh specialises in leadership and organisational development, particularly at the nexus of inclusion, psychological safety and performance. Sile also brings expertise in coaching psychology and organisational development. With more than a decade of experience serving clients in Ireland and abroad, her mission is to strengthen impactful leadership to cultivate high-performance, inclusive environments where individuals thrive and great work gets done! Located in Dublin, she operates both locally and globally, offering her services in-person and online.

Sile is in her fourth year of a PhD in Professional Practice: Psychological Studies at Canterbury Christ Church University, focusing on inclusive leadership in the school of applied psychology. She holds a HDip in Coaching Psychology and an MSc in Personal and Management Coaching from University College Cork, along with additional certifications in Leadership, Participatory Management and Professional Supervision.

Sile's commitment to trauma-informed and inclusive practices originates from her diverse experiences working with various marginalised communities, including those with mental ill health challenges, addiction recovery, engaged in the criminal justice system, LGBTQ+ community and others facing systemic barriers.

Sile excels in designing, training, and supervising programs for charities and private organisations. With extensive community experience, she values ongoing personal therapy, coaching and professional development in her role as a coach and practitioner.

SWAN - Start With A Name

My Name is Síle Walsh. It is an Irish spelling name, and it was chosen in honour of my paternal grandmother.

Phonetically in English Síle is pronounced She-la, and Walsh is pronounced Wal-shh.

Since beginning to work internationally, I have spelt my name as Sile Walsh and removed the beloved fada. This decision, born from practicality, ensures my name is clear across cultures even when it is mispronounced as Tile but with an S.

I share this because a campaign called "SWAN", which means "starts with a name", has had a big impact on my professional practice, both in terms of having my name pronounced correctly and, even more so, in terms of ensuring that I can pronounce others' names correctly.

DEDICATION

This work is dedicated to everyone who has carried the baton before me, to every individual who chooses to delve into these pages with me, and to those who accompany us on this journey in parallel efforts.

Each contributes in their unique manner, breathing life into it in their unique ways; there is not one way, there are many, and it is these many ways that will maintain the richness of uniqueness and the skill of belonging.

It is a homage to all of us: those who came before, those among us now, and those who will join us in the future.

CONTENTS

FOREWORD

I have held leadership roles for decades, and from the first page of this book, I was engaged, my curiosity about the topic was piqued and I quickly began to evaluate my own practice. Inclusive Leadership is a lively and progressive take that reflects Sile's expertise and knowledge in this subject area. I am fortunate to know Sile, for many years now and have had the chance to deliver some programmes with her. I learn something new from Sile, every time I meet her. When I bumped into Sile in an airport in Scotland and she told me she was writing a book on inclusive leadership, I knew that it would be intriguing, thought provoking and full of real-world insights. Indeed, that is exactly what this book is. It made me think. It challenged me and it offered me perspectives I had not previously considered.

In Inclusive Leadership, Sile states, that it is easy to discuss inclusion, to promote it. It's another thing to practice it. While this book examines the complexity of inclusion, it is presented in a way that helps to simplify one's thinking. The inclusive leadership insights provided throughout the book create an overall framework that helps readers to evaluate their current approaches or their aspirational goals for embedding inclusive practices in leadership or at an organisational level. These insights are primarily drawn from Sile's direct personal and professional experience. She openly shares many examples of learning the hard way. This honesty provides the reader with a reassurance that embarking on an inclusive leadership journey will have bumpy patches. To manage this, Sile provides very practical tools and frameworks to help with a wide array of issues.

The examples used in this book are relevant to today, which makes it easy for the reader to apply the content to their own contexts, no matter how diverse these may be. For me, there were many "aha" moments in this book, such as those that pointed how to continue to evolve and deepen leadership practice. I also valued the questions asked in the book that encouraged me to consider what else I can do to increase the likelihood of creating a sustainable, inclusive organisation.

While I read this book with my own practice in mind, I noticed that the focus of the content shifted from that of leadership practice to enhancing the organisational environment. This is particularly useful, as it provides a challenge to leaders to think, not just about themselves but about inclusion from operational and strategic perspectives, including policies and procedures, practice (at all levels of the organisation), reward, attraction, retention, senior leadership and even governance. This holistic view is refreshing and useful regardless of whether you are a leader, an influencer, a champion, a HR or OD professional. This book does not show you how to tick the box regarding inclusion and diversity, instead it encourages thoughtful reflection, planning, application, and evaluation for meaningful and sustainable progress.

Sile highlights the link between effective inclusive leadership and positive organisational performance. She also explains the risks both to the organisation and to individuals of ignoring inclusion or getting it wrong. Sile comes on the journey with you. Through the unique practical dimension to this book, tools, frameworks and checklists are provided to support critical thinking, this makes the content relevant to those at various stages of the journey to greater inclusivity.

Through knowing and working with Sile I have experienced inclusive leadership. Sile demonstrates authentic inclusive leadership in her day-to-day interactions and through this book, she has generously shared her insights and intelligence, acquired over many years. Readers will gain a deeper understanding of what inclusive leadership is and what it is not. There are so many practical tools to choose from, which will help plan positive leadership or organisational change as well as broadening readers minds and skill sets. The examples are relevant and delivered with Siles sense of humour, which helps the reader to realise that the journey to effective inclusive leadership is challenging, yet the reward is immense for all.

PREFACE

Inclusive Leadership: Navigating Organisational Complexity is a guide dedicated to enhancing individual, team, and organisational performance rather than detracting from it. It shifts the focus from merely adding tasks to improving processes and practices for more effective outcomes.

Sile Walsh offers a fresh perspective on inclusion, portraying it as essential for every individual to thrive and perform within organisations. By reframing inclusion as a set of principles rather than rules, she leads readers from a mindset of fear to one of freedom and from survival to flourishing.

This book is indispensable for leaders and HR professionals committed to enacting real change within their organisations. By integrating relational, psychological, and performance-based approaches, readers are empowered to lead inclusively, drive organisational excellence, and attain sustainable success.

Discover a transformative journey towards fostering psychologically safe, inclusive, and high-performing teams and organisations by learning the 13 *Inclusive Leadership Principles* within this book. Uncover strategies for enhancing performance and organisational excellence, navigate diversity and inclusion challenges, leverage inclusive leadership tools, and embed inclusive practices into organisational culture for lasting results.

I would love you to interact with me about the book and your journey with it across social media sites. Tag @SileWalsh1 and use #ILNOC to share your thoughts and see what others are saying!

To download any supports or resources across the book, visit www.silewalsh.com/ilnoc-resources

PART 1:
SURVEYING
THE LANDSCAPE

CHAPTER 1: CURIOSITY KILLED THE CAT

> *"You think the only people who are people, are the people who look and think like you. But if you walk the footsteps of a stranger, you'll learn things you never knew, you never knew."*
>
> — Judy Kuhn

When I was nine, I got into trouble because I kept asking questions in school. The principal informed my parents and asked them to tell me to stop. So, they did. They already had nine years of my questions, and I reckon they could resonate with his frustration.

The irony was that a week later, I got the highest school results for my class for the national maths exams. The principal responded by telling the class, "See, be more like Sile. Ask questions if you don't understand something." I remember it vividly as it was the only experience I ever had of anything positive being said publicly about my academic abilities during my school days.

Everything else was always, "Try harder. You will figure it out," and "Practice more." There was an assumption that I didn't comprehend what they were teaching.

At least, that's how I remember it, but even now, when writing this, I doubt myself because I never got to be the highest in anything in life. In retrospect, this may have also been the week I started to think I would like to be a maths professor, and that became my new answer to "What would you like to be when you grow up?" for the approaching year. That was until I realised I was terrible at showing how I worked out my solutions in maths. Apparently, it's important to not just have the right answer but evidence of how you found it.

My brain has always been curious. If I could turn it off, I would. It annoys people because I don't accept one point of view. I ask why when others wish I wouldn't. I wake up at night with Aha moments and think of existential questions that grip me for days, weeks, and often years. I can argue against everything I believe in because I am so curious. I even want to know how I might be wrong. This curiosity leads me to value things differently, to not assume that what one person or their group values is more important than another and vice versa. This means I don't easily agree with group dynamics or fit into them.

"To have moral courage is to challenge conformity within our own tribes—be they religious, cultural, ideological, or professional—and to do so for a more universal good."

— Irshad Manji

Over the years, I have seen my curiosity go beyond what people say or do and into how they interact with power. What power dynamics are they inviting me into, and what power dynamics am I inviting others into?

A fundamental underlying curiosity about the power I engage with prevents me from thinking anything is one-dimensional. Inclusive leadership is not just what I say and do but also how I use my power in the things I say and do.

I constantly attempt to align and realign with the idea that the violation of human rights by anyone, to anyone, is fundamentally not ok. You might think, "Yeah, obviously," but that is not always the case. Stick with me a moment.

Inclusive leadership has to have some relationship with a wider social lens. For me, human rights are as good as any. Most people agree theoretically with me on this until their ideas of whose rights are more important than others come into play. This is where power starts to enact power struggles, and winning something distorts our relationship with human rights.

In my thinking and understanding of the issue, human rights supersede all else at any time, anywhere, by anyone, and to anyone. I do not care about the laws, the political agendas, if I am aligned with the perpetrator or the victim, or whether I understand the person's experience or not. I do not count one human right or one person as more important than another. I constantly hold these tensions in my thoughts, work, and process. It would be so much easier not to, but to me, it would be lazy and self-serving.

So, when I speak about inclusive leadership, I am not speaking about only including those I agree with. I am speaking about leading in a way that all people are enabled to belong and be valued for their uniqueness within the confines of organisational boundaries.

Human rights, as defined by the United Nations (UN), is a guiding set of principles I liaise with within my comprehension and critical thinking, and it is often why I don't sit firmly in any camp of political thought. I feel most camps of thought strive to hold political power (whether conscious or unconscious) and not uphold human rights and the dignity of all.

This is fundamental throughout in and out group norms, so you will find challenges, ideas, alignment, and provocation dispersed within these pages. You will find invitations or opportunities, but you will not find the valuing of the rights of one person above another. You will not observe the promotion of trendy topics of inclusion or a political ideology. You will not see the reduction of people to one part of their identity. You will find the conversation speaks from multiple perspectives, holding complexity as a valid part of organisational life and, therefore, leadership. You will uncover discussions about power and the different ways power is enhancing and hindering inclusive leadership.

You will find my exploration and my ideas, conversations I want you to think about and things I am currently thinking about, but you will not find me telling you what way to think.

Curiosity may have killed the cat, yet I don't know how to live any other way, and I don't want to.

Positionality is an essential insight in research. As I am doing a PhD on inclusive leadership, it is clear that my positionality is relevant to all of my work.

I want to start by inviting you to consider your position.

Positionality is your starting point, at which you view your topic from your experience and how your experiences and identities have impacted how you approach a subject, including how you read this book.

However, before I could invite anybody else to do that, I must start with my own positionality. In actual fact, sharing my own makes me nervous.

As a coach, I often do not discuss my identity because it is not about me but the client. While I don't believe I can be neutral, I use the space between the client and myself as a space for the client so that they can fill it with their points of view and perspectives and unpack them in a way that helps them achieve what they want from their lives and work. They bring whatever they need into that space so they can move forward. They do this without judgement from me. Instead, I seek to understand them and their beliefs from their perspective as best I can.

Image management is something we all do, whether we are aware of it or not. If my coaching clients have to hide parts of themselves because of the projections they may have related to my identity or my political position, then my identity, politics, and all the projections that come with it become a barrier to the coaching process. Although my identity remains constant, there are instances where it may be beneficial for clients to focus on their own journey rather than on aspects of my identity that are not readily visible. This can help them stay connected to their personal growth process.

However, my positionality and aspects of my identity are vital in researching, working with organisations, and consulting on leadership, inclusion, and organisational development. I need to share where I stand and help those I am working with understand how I am listening and what lenses I am considering.

I need to be clear. I do not judge the clients I work with for any isms or phobias they may or may not share. While I have done much work to unpack these things within myself, this work never ends for me. This is not only because my coaching psychology practice is non-judgemental but also because I am not better than anyone else, regardless of their beliefs or my own.

I do not judge them for representing something that makes sense to them and their worldview, even if I have a different worldview. They have experienced different things within society, which has led them to their positionality, as is true for all of us.

I acknowledge that we are born into systems with many isms and phobias built into who and what we value. Therefore, all of us are impacted by these and often internalise them unconsciously.

While I do everything to unwrap mine consciously, I also acknowledge that on any given day, I can find out that something I am saying, thinking, believing, or doing is any of those isms or phobias, and I am not above that. It is an ongoing process.

However, in coaching, when somebody works with me, they come to me for support and guidance. They set the scene and the content, and I do not believe it is my place to insert my beliefs or values into our work together. I believe that if what they are presenting relates to the challenges they employed me to help them with, I can show those links and demonstrate the connections. However, I have to take a moment to ask myself in this coaching relationship to identify if this is my place, and at times, it is not. I often spend time reflecting afterwards, bringing these tensions and reflections to supervision, and asking myself existential questions about my role, the purpose of our work, the agreement we have in place, and what all that means.

Presume you are going to try to work with people through transformation in your workplace. In that case, you need to understand that all of these isms and phobias exist in society and, therefore, exist within the psyche of every one of us in some way and in our organisations.

To judge it or to have it as a mission to change another person's mindset or experience that is outside of what they have contracted me to do is oppressive, and that is my starting point. I believe in the coaching process. I believe my role as a coach is important, and holding that space creates transformation.

When I am hired to consult or to work with organisations or individuals around inclusion, they have employed me to identify these things and to discuss them with the organisation, which means my positionality becomes essential. They need to know where I stand when I make these assertions, comments, or points of view. They also need to know that if what we discuss becomes any of these isms or phobias or continued oppression, I can explain the issue to them without judgement. I can say what I see without judging others or becoming superior to them.

Being without judgement here is essential. I honestly believe that if I am going to work with people and help transform workplaces into inclusive environments, I have to be able to sit and respect people who have wildly different beliefs and values from me. This is not always easy, but it is a practice I am committed to fail at often and, at other times, succeed with ease.

Otherwise, what I am trying to do is oppress and dominate others with my values and beliefs.

This implies that when faced with someone who dehumanises either my own identity, the identity of a loved one, or anyone else's identity, I need to navigate a delicate balance. I need to refrain from dominating or oppressing them, even as they may consciously or unconsciously attempt to dominate or oppress me.

I need to consider all this while also knowing that they have hired me in the consulting role and that I have a responsibility to discuss our responsibilities within the workplace towards an inclusive environment and inclusive leadership. This means identifying things that are isms or phobias without shaming or blaming individuals who are replicating these systemic patterns.

This is even harder for me and others when the person is actively dehumanising us, whether they are aware or not.

I honestly believe that when one of us dehumanises another in any way, we are inherently dehumanising ourselves. If I perceive someone as inferior for any reason, it implies that I believe if I were associated with that identity, I would also be inferior. It suggests that if I were born into a different family, race, gender, religion, time zone, geography, or year, my inherent worth would be diminished.

I do not look at others who have these beliefs as bad people. Firstly, because I know that I also have these beliefs, which are often unconscious and when they do become conscious, I do my best to work on them. However, I know that I am no better than anybody else. I also know that we hold our own beliefs and values based on our lived experience, which is valid for everyone.

Our lived experiences inform how we see the world, and therefore, how can I decide that my way of seeing the world is true or that the other person is wrong?

Despite the fact perceptions of the world are made up of subjective experiences, we often assume that our way of viewing the world is true. Therefore, it can be difficult to hold the idea that our experience is our truth and not everyone else's. This means that when we sit with our experience and truth, we also need to sit with and hold other people's experiences and truth at the same time. This thought process comes from some of the work of Myira Khan, who talks about anti-oppressive practice (Khan, 2023) in her book *Working Within Diversity*, which I highly recommend. Beyond that, I also think about what is helpful or unhelpful or what is harmful or not harmful. I do not believe it is possible not to be harmful in this world. Harm is, unfortunately, part of the human experience. But I believe we can be less harmful and act in a way that reduces harm and focuses on being helpful.

I do not view people with wildly different beliefs as less than me. I may, like all of us, struggle with them when they challenge my humanity or when they attempt to use power over me through dominant or oppressive approaches. Nevertheless, I do not see them as less than others. I see them as equal human beings who see the world through a particular lens for whatever reason. Some of those reasons I may not understand, others I will.

My position is unique in that I wish for an inclusive world where all people are included and can thrive in our societies and workplaces. I am also aware that we live within systems of capitalism, racism, classism, ageism, ableism, religious discrimination, and different engagements of power and privilege. It can be tough to create an inclusive society.

One of the ways I try to do this is by supporting organisations to have more inclusive workplaces. By fostering more inclusive environments, individuals can enhance their experiences of differences and promote collaboration among people with varied backgrounds and perspectives. This increased tolerance for difference in the workplace can later extend into society, potentially offering more beneficial outcomes than our current methods achieve. This is often a positive and unintended consequence that clients and students report to me after engaging in inclusive leadership development and an improvement in relationships and awareness.

Power and Privilege

There are parts of my identity that are more easily visible, such as my race, age, and sex. I am a native English speaker, and because I openly discuss it in my work and life, it is known that I am dyslexic.

These are the first parts of my identity most people see or are aware of. Other parts of my identity are less visible.

This will also be a reality for you, and some of the visible aspects of your identity will serve as barriers or give you experiences you would prefer not to have. Often, we refer to this as marginalisation, bias, or discrimination. Nevertheless, you will likely have a visible aspect of your identity, often referred to as power and privilege, which doesn't result in barriers, marginalisation, and discrimination. In fact, it may result in an ease that others do not have.

I employ the terms power and privilege because they are commonly recognised, but my belief extends beyond mere acknowledgement. I genuinely advocate for the privileges enjoyed by some to be regarded as a benchmark for universal human experience rather than sources of shame. I perceive them as standards to aspire to, especially for those who currently lack access to them.

Most people hold both power and privilege with some of the aspects of their identity while also possibly experiencing disadvantages for other aspects of their identity. One does not negate the other, as the work of Myira Khan discusses.

My Positionality

My positionality here matters. It matters why I write this book and how all my whys lead to the positions I take on these pages. I disclose the aspects of my positionality that shape this book. However, it's important to note that no positionality statement can encompass my entirety, including all my identities and experiences of power or marginalisation. The ones detailed here are the primary influences on this work.

I am dyslexic, and that is my first overt experience of difference. What do I mean by that? It was the first time I had a name for the difference I was experiencing. I was about thirteen when I first came across this explanation for my experiences.

This is not my first experience of othering, difference, or marginalisation, but it is my first experience of having a term for it. When people found out I was dyslexic, they felt sorry for me, and it became clear that some peers felt shame about being dyslexic. Dyslexia shapes a lot of how I succeed in the world, but it also shapes a lot of how systems are not designed for me.

Before this term and official diagnosis, I had other experiences of difference. I was born in the UK and grew up in Ireland. I was always too much of one thing and not enough of another, caught between a strong Irish identity and an English accent.

I come from a working-class family, and with it comes intergenerational challenges and strengths. This expresses itself in different ways every day. My working-class background and my family, who I class as "good people" (good people meaning that they are solid, good-intentioned, hard-working, compassionate people. Not that they are perfect!) instilled hard work in me. They valued education and for us to contribute to our communities in different ways.

I grew up having people over to our home for Christmas dinner because they would be alone otherwise. My parents, aunts, and uncles volunteered for different activities to support others. I remember when I was ten, I said to my dad, "We better lock the car door. Someone might steal our shopping." I had my favourite sweets in the bag with the bread and ham for lunches. I was not keen to lose those sweets. He replied, "If someone steals our bread, they need it more than we do." I wasn't worried about the bread but about my blackjacks. We left the car door unlocked, and thankfully, when we returned, no one needed them more than we did!

Often, my family supported other people, and I was encouraged to support others when life was difficult for them for various reasons. We were also supported by many others when we needed help. This was all a normal part of my life growing up. It wasn't something I thought was unusual or made us better than others. I really believed this was how all humans functioned, and I guess this is why I was naive in a number of professional agreements later on in life, but that is for another story.

I didn't see us as superior or inferior to others. Rather, I viewed it as a shared responsibility to address the unmet needs of those within our reach. This mindset greatly shaped my self-perception and relationship with others, and it still does.

As a white woman, I benefit from the privilege of being white, which shields me from certain barriers. However, my experience as a woman has exposed me to numerous instances of misogyny, sexism, and harmful attitudes, particularly because I have worked in male-dominated environments since the age of eleven.

This means that toxic masculinity was normalised in these environments, and I had to manage this norm. I also want to say that in these environments, I met supportive, helpful, encouraging, and empowering people, as well as the opposite. While I think it would be unfair to say that I come from a poor background, it is important to say I come from a background that did not have a lot of financial security, and both my parents needed to work at different times to ensure we weren't stuck. They didn't have the privilege of extended time off without a lot of stress. However, we did have meaningful relationships and we learned to give and receive gracefully, which is one of my favourite qualities in a person to date – generosity. This influenced my relationship with money but also my understanding of class.

From the age of eleven, I worked with very wealthy people and those from every class identity from the underclass (I dislike this term, but it's the current one used. I prefer the phrase "under-served class"), working class, middle class, and upper class. I had exposure to a variety of people from different classes with very different financial security. This is one of the reasons I am so clear that class matters in a way that others who have not experienced it might not understand. I only learned about class when I started babysitting on the side for very wealthy families and minding upper-middle-class children. The differences were stark from what I had experienced in my own community. I learned that class was a thing, and I began to see differences in security, networks, expectations, opportunities, and support.

At the age of eighteen, I also started to travel. I spent several years going back and forth to India, practising and seeing different spiritual practices, exploring Hinduism, considering Christianity differently, and thinking about Islam. I developed a spiritual practice in my life, which I have since normalised and integrated into a much more practical way of being. What I mean by this is that I do not think my religion or spirituality is anything about where I pray or who I pray to. It is more about how I treat others and engage in the world. I cannot say that this is not directly linked to my work and inclusion because inclusion, to me, is ultimately about practising my own spiritual beliefs. These include the idea that humanity can be better to each other and that our spirituality is not based on our beliefs, practices, or traditions but on our way of treating each other.

My spirituality is in how I treat and engage with others, and for me, this is much more important. I have sat in the ashrams. I have engaged in silent retreats. I learned mindfulness before it became globally recognised. I engaged in energy and healing work and considered all the things that come with that sphere. Within it, I found much spirituality bypassing in myself, and, at times, in others, I found many replications of isms dressed up and excused as gurus, wise people, and influencers. So much so that now I engage with spirituality as being about integration, understanding, compassion, and leaving the world better than I found it, if at all possible.

While there are other aspects of my identity that inform my work, my life, and my way of being, these are the ones that really embedded a value of inclusion long before I would ever know the term or that society would speak about it so widely. These are the foundations of how I am in the world and how I came to write *Inclusive Leadership: Navigating Organisational Complexity.*

Before we move forward, I encourage you to consider your position and reflect on any three of these questions:

    »   What brings you here to read this book?
    »   What fundamental experiences shape your relationship with inclusive leadership?
    »   How do you relate to others with differing views?
    »   How do you feel about this being ongoing and never concluded?

» How do you feel about the idea that if furthering your values and beliefs requires you to use power over another, that this may be oppressive?
» How does it feel to sit with yourself, fully, beautifully, human and flawed and be as much a part of the problem as the solution?
» What do you need to be okay within your positionality as it is now?
» What do you need to sit with others?
» Do some of the above identities I share provoke assumptions in you?
» What identities do you give more power to than others?

> *"Every journey starts with the first step."*
>
> — My dad (adapted from Lao Tzu)

The journey in inclusive leadership is never-ending, and I highly recommend you read this with that in mind. Otherwise, you will want to do everything at once and easily find yourself overwhelmed. Take the next best step rather than choose to be frozen in fear or overwhelm. Progress is what we aim for here, not perfection.

Within these pages, I have quotes that resonate with me. Some are from unknown contributors, some are familiar phrases, and some are from different religious scriptures. I share these as I find they encapsulate points I have not been able to explain better. However, please know I am not suggesting that religion or spirituality is required to be inclusive or an inclusive leader. I am simply sharing from the diverse set of resources I lean into when reflecting on inclusive leadership and from which I have compiled this book.

I have met as many effective leaders who have no spiritual beliefs as those with spiritual beliefs. I have also met as many ineffective leaders with spiritual beliefs as those without spiritual beliefs. I have met as many marginalised folks who are not inclusive leaders as I have those who are. I have met as many non-marginalised folks who are not inclusive leaders as I have those who are.

Inclusive leadership is a practice, not a belief.

It is a practice, not an identity.

It is a practice, not something to be achieved. It is something we practice.

> "Education is not just about filling up a pail; it's about lighting a fire."
>
> — Michael D Higgins

In reading so many leadership books and discussing these with my leadership book club, I became aware of how much we perpetuate a very limited view of leadership, which has a direct dotted line to heroism and individualism. While these words are for individuals to read, they will flourish differently depending on the collective needs that are within your reality. This book is an invitation. Do with it as you will.

"We need to strive for a society where everyone has equal opportunities to reach their full potential. We need to strive for a society where everyone has equal opportunities to reach their full potential."

— Mary McAleese

PART 2:
LAYING THE FOUNDATIONS

Setting the Stage for Leadership Transformation

It is easy to assume we know what we are talking about. One of the assumptions I had when starting my PhD and from talking with professionals in the field of inclusion was that we understood what we spoke about. The issue with this is that we may all be talking about the same thing, conceptualising it differently, and considering success from different points.

After thousands of conversations with leaders, I realised that assumptions and misinterpretations are some of the biggest barriers to transformation in organisations.

As you delve into each chapter, my intention is for readers to start from a common understanding, enabling us to think collectively rather than diverging in separate directions. While it is not necessary for us to hold identical perspectives, it's crucial to avoid misinterpretations that could lead us astray from mutual comprehension.

When asked what quote gives you hope, my brother suggested this one, and I feel it is a great way to begin reading this book.

> *"Our deepest fear is not that we are inadequate. Our deepest fear is that we are powerful beyond measure. It is our light, not our darkness, that most frightens us. We ask ourselves, who am I to be brilliant, gorgeous, talented, fabulous? Actually, who are you not to be? You are a child of God. Your playing small does not serve the World. There is nothing enlightening about shrinking so that other people won't feel unsure around you. We were born to make manifest the glory of God that is within us. It is not just in some of us; it's in everyone. As we let our own light shine, we consciously give other people permission to do the same. As we are liberated from our own fear, our presence automatically liberates others."*
>
> — Marianne Williamson, *A Return to Love* (1992)

CHAPTER 2: CAN WE START WHERE WE REALLY ARE?

One of the many questions I get asked when I start speaking about inclusive leadership is, "Can you define it?" At first, I was surprised at how frequently this question came up, but as time went on, I realised that inclusion is not as simple to agree on as we think.

Additionally, when I look at the commercial side of inclusive leadership and academic research, it is really evident why people ask this question. We use the term as if it has a global meaning, and yet its meaning differs drastically from person to person. It is best to start with a clear definition of inclusive leadership rather than assumptions.

> *"Inclusive leadership is the effective use of inclusion practices in all forms of leadership, whether positional, thought, or social leadership, throughout an organisation with the purpose of co-creating an inclusive, psychologically safe, high-performing organisation."*

— Sile Walsh, 2022

Inclusion practices refer to fostering and facilitating the perception of belonging and uniqueness (Shore et al., 2011) with group members. However, it's important to know that a feeling of not belonging does not require a slight, but it can sit in the environment with subtle cues of one's identity not being compatible (Slepian & Jacoby-Senghor, 2020). When I say different forms of leadership, formal leadership refers to leadership where one occupies an organisational leadership position. When I refer to the leaders in your organisation who influence others through their thought leadership and social leaders who influence people through social relationships, I refer to informal leadership. Which is often not understood or respected as much as formal leadership due to our history of "hero" leadership seeping into our concept of good leaders.

It is essential to note that often, when we think about inclusion and inclusive leadership, we are thinking about it through a societal lens. This means that we consider political leaders and leadership much broader than organisational leadership. Societal leadership is often about justice, politics, and societal equality. However, in organisations, there are very real boundaries to the remit of leaders. We need to consider the purpose of inclusive leadership in organisations in more depth. For this reason, we need to break inclusive leadership down further than the general widespread consensus about inclusive leadership and inclusive society.

Inclusive Leadership Insight 1: There are three types of leaders when it comes to inclusive leadership in organisations: formal leaders with positional titles and informal leaders who lead through either social leadership approaches or thought leadership approaches.

We need first to decide what inclusive leadership is. Is it more about inclusion or more about leadership? Is inclusive leadership something completely different?

This might sound pedantic, but it is essential. In the work and research I am doing as a coach, leadership educator, and consultant, I have found that the starting point either sets us up to succeed or fail.

I am going to share some definitions that I utilise and that we will be discussing throughout the book. The first thing to note is that inclusive leadership, as with all organisational leadership, has to serve the organisation's purpose. If it does not serve the organisation's purpose, it usually becomes an add-on or a *nice to have something* or extra. Furthermore, if we think about leadership, defining it is essential. In my work, I have found that over the years of working with leaders from multiple settings, leadership often has a very restricted understanding or definition based on how the organisation discusses it.

Inclusive Leadership Insight 2: Inclusive leadership needs to serve the organisational purpose to become embedded and be sustainable.

When I speak about inclusive leadership, I first speak about leaders in formal positions, thought leaders and social leaders. I am also thinking about leadership from a social construct, meaning that I am thinking about leadership through the lens of followership. You cannot lead without followers.

Followers do not mean that you are ahead or that followers are submissive, but followers may refer to people leaning into your opinions, ideas, ways of being, and suggestions. Followers mean they opt into engaging with your leadership. Basically, they trust your influence in some way and, therefore, give you followership.

I use the example of a dinner party to explain followership so that people do not think I am discussing dominance and submissiveness. At the dinner party, the host represents the leader, the guest the followers. The host sets up the dinner party. That's their role, and the guests attend. Everything that makes the party a success is down to how the host and guest interact, share power, and engage with their role at the party.

- Does the host check the availability of guests?
- Does the host facilitate suggestions for food?
- Do the guests forget to RSVP?
- Do either turn up late?
- Do the guests avoid engaging with prepping and then complain about the host's choices?
- Do guests see their role as passive or as active?

- Does the host see their role as dominating or facilitating good conversations?

The understanding of followership is often misunderstood as always agreeable or powerless. However, leadership is a reciprocal relationship with followership. Neither is an identity. They are roles we fulfil as needed and roles an inclusive leader needs to be able to provoke in others and fulfil themselves.

Positional leadership is more challenging for followership because you may have to follow where somebody is going and be influenced by them. However, it may not be something you would choose if your career, role, or job were not dependent on it. Followership is not always about preference or following people we like or agree with. Sometimes, it is about following the direction that an organisation or leader is bringing us because our role only exists to ultimately facilitate the purpose of the organisation.

Inclusive Leadership Insight 3: You cannot lead as an inclusive leader without a reciprocal dynamic with your followership.

I define inclusion through a scientific measure, which, simply put, is the facilitation of belonging and uniqueness (Shore et al., 2011). However, do not overemphasise belonging, which I find many organisations currently do. If we have too much belonging, we will be out of balance and may recreate cliques in groups and assimilation. There is a need to balance belonging with uniqueness, which is often discussed as differences and diversity. Uniqueness is the ability to feel that I have value to add here in an organisation that is different to others. In an organisation, inclusion is not the same as in a society. Belonging in an organisation is how I contribute to the organisation, whereas in a society, it is a right.

Do I have a place here? Do I belong in this organisation? If belonging is related to my place in the organisation, then I belong by contributing to the organisation's purpose in a particular way.

The uniqueness is that I can be myself to an appropriate degree for this setting, which means I can support the organisation in achieving its goals. I can also think about my unique perspectives, lived experiences, and differences and how these could add value and create more of a robust understanding of the organisational goal.

Inclusive Leadership Insight 4: Inclusion is the experience of belonging and uniqueness in a workgroup. Being inclusive is inviting people into the group dynamic to be themselves.

It is essential to remember that sometimes people say we should be our authentic selves at work. It is important to note that this is not helpful and practically cannot be accurate. From a psychological lens, we are never fully our authentic selves in any setting. While we might bring our authentic selves to the setting, expressing that part of ourselves may not be appropriate. In diversity and inclusion work, it's important to recognise that having to hide or mask parts of our identity doesn't promote inclusion or performance at work.

When we mask parts of our identity, it takes extra energy and effort, which can become a challenge when contributing to the task at hand. So, I want to separate those two ideas as well. Authenticity is due to having a strong connection with myself. However, in the workplace, we may not want to bring our whole selves to work in the way that people would like us to.

For instance, I do not have the same conversations with a niece or nephew as I do with a partner, and I do not have the same conversations with my therapist as I do at family dinners. This is not because I am inauthentic. It is because authenticity is our relationship with ourselves and what aspects we wish to share. But in any environment, in any relationship, group or organisation, there is context. We need to decide what is appropriate for that context. This is not about being inauthentic. It is about knowing that our authenticity is something we have a relationship with within ourselves. However, in the workplace, we need to decide what parts of our authenticity and what parts of ourselves we will bring into that setting.

A lot of discrimination legislation is based on ensuring we are not mistreated or need to hide certain parts of ourselves. If I have to hide a part of my identity, it might be because there is a risk in some form to how I will be seen, treated, or even from a safety perspective, depending on where you are in the world and the culture of the organisation. So much work around diversity and inclusion in organisations is linked to or motivated by anti-discrimination. The legislation is really coming from the idea that masking aspects of your identity is not required or equitable in the workplace. You should not need to do it. We do not want people to wear a mask or code switch or hide who they are. However, that doesn't mean that every part of everyone's

31

identity needs to be expressed and experienced in the workplace.

However, your authenticity, values, and morals are not always the most helpful things to bring into the workplace for many different reasons. I am not suggesting that you should be inauthentic or not use your values or morals to guide you. I am suggesting that if you are using your values, morals, and authenticity as an expectation of how others should be, you will have an issue in the workplace. The workplace is primarily a place to work. Shared work is what brings us together. While it can be a place where many people derive value, a sense of achievement, community and connection, its primary purpose is to contribute to the work purpose.

Currently, I see an increase in the expectation of a workplace to meet every need a person may have. An idea that work is where I should be able to be everything I am. However, that is not the case. In reality, the workplace and organisation only exist due to the shared purpose of the organisation's end goals.

For instance, no one wants to hear me sing karaoke at work, but it might be the perfect activity in a social setting. *(FYI, it is never a good time for me to sing! But hopefully, you get the gist.)*

Work is, first and foremost, a place for producing an organisational outcome. Additionally, it might be a place where we can express different parts of ourselves appropriately on occasion.

It shouldn't be a place where we have to mask or hide aspects of our identity; however, that is very different from the notion of "bring your whole self to work" or "I am just being authentic."

Inclusive Leadership Insight 5: There is a difference between authenticity and masking at work. We need to reduce the need for masking at work and not get distracted by getting our whole identity met at work.

This is why discrimination law and inclusion are really different. Inclusion cannot be mandated. It is an ongoing social process. Even if you design an invitation to include people or facilitate inclusion, people have the right to decline it. It is just an invitation. Individuals have the right to express statements and sentiments of, "I prefer not to disclose my sexual orientation," or "I choose not to discuss my religious beliefs," or "I'm not comfortable discussing my gender identity," or "I prefer not to be associated with that particular group."

Because organisations and societies are collapsing the idea of inclusion in organisations, societal inclusion, and discrimination, there is a misunderstanding and a misalignment with expectations. We all enter the workplace primarily to support the tasks of the organisation. That is the purpose of our work and the purpose of our place in the workplace. The workplace has obligations and responsibilities to you, as an employee and as a member of that organisation, and you have obligations to the workplace and your colleagues. However, we need to be careful about collapsing the expectations we have of society into organisations as if they are equivalent. Rather, they are related and intertwined but also distinctive and different in boundaries and practicalities.

We do not usually get to pick the society that we are part of. We don't have the choice to participate or abstain. We belong there, and society has an obligation to all its people. However, we only join an organisation because we can contribute to its purpose. So, inclusion and inclusive leadership have to lean on supporting the organisation to succeed by integrating inclusive practices rather than attempting to correct society through inclusion efforts. *(Don't get me wrong here. I want an inclusive society. However, this collapse is only furthering polarisation and causing ineffective approaches to inclusion in organisations.)*

There also needs to be an understanding that people need to be supported so that they do not have to mask or hide aspects of themselves. We have to be really clear, though. Inclusive leadership within an organisation is about supporting organisations by including members and supporting their performance. At both individual and organisational levels, employing inclusive practices is essential.

For example, I cannot decide that I am going to join a legal firm if I do not have a legal qualification. I cannot say, "You are excluding me." It is true that they are excluding me, but they are excluding me in alignment with the purpose of the organisation.

This is also true of how we manifest and create inclusion within any organisation. We need to consider the purpose of the organisation, organisational strategy, vision, values, and mission. All of these things have to influence inclusion. That is why a standardised approach to inclusive leadership or organisational inclusion is not helpful. Its starting point already distracts from the purpose of inclusive leadership, which is to support the organisation in thriving. Hence, we need to start with what the organisation needs to succeed and co-create the approach from there.

There are far too many approaches simply replicating what is being done in other organisations, usually out of fear of getting it wrong, but this approach is a limitation. You know the saying, "Oh yeah, you do everything your friends do, do you?" Well, I can hear my mother saying this when I see the replication process happening. Instead of replicating, conduct a proper needs analysis and see how inclusive leadership can support your biggest challenges.

Inclusive Leadership Insight 6: Inclusion in organisations has limitations by the purpose of the organisation.

It is important to think about whether we are thinking about inclusion and inclusive leadership as something that is morally good. Often, I have found that in practice, when you think about it as something that is morally good, we tend to unconsciously have rules about who should and should not be included. *"Bring your authentic self to work as long as it isn't racist, homophobic, or ablest."*

In my experience working with leaders and discussing inclusion, it's clear that inclusive leadership means collaborating effectively with people who differ from you in various aspects, including identity, values, principles, practices, visions, missions, and political viewpoints.

In the workplace, debating such matters may not be helpful. However, limiting inclusion to those similar to oneself perpetuates ingroup-outgroup dynamics, presenting a longstanding challenge to true inclusion.

Inclusion is not natural or automatic. That does not mean we should not do it. There are lots of things that are not natural or automatic that are very helpful for us in our lives. Inclusion requires intentional effort. Our natural instinct and automatic responses around group dynamics is to find people like us and who agree with us.

Inclusion invites us to go beyond that to broaden our capacity for understanding and tolerating differences and leveraging those tolerances to improve our performance at work individually and as a group.

Inclusive Leadership Insight 7: Inclusion invites us to learn to work with those different to us across all spectrums of differences.

Inclusive leadership is about how you include others and make room for differences, not just identity. It is about how you regulate yourself when you disagree with somebody. It's about engaging in conversations while also acknowledging the unknown, challenging your own assumptions and being open to reconsidering what you might believe to be true or universal is, in fact, not true and universal for everyone.

Inclusive Leadership Insight 8: Inclusive leadership is all about how we do things.

It's also about inviting in more space and critical thinking, not just considering who we include but what we include.

What conversations are we having or not having? What data are we valuing or devaluing? Not just who, but what? And so, throughout this book, you will find that I talk a lot about inclusive leadership in much broader ways than we have traditionally talked about it up to now.

I do this not to confuse or avoid taking a stance but because inclusive leadership entails understanding oneself, including biases, and actively making necessary changes.

Inclusive Leadership Insight 9: Inclusive leadership is about considering who and what we include.

Inclusive leadership within organisations has boundaries and is not just about promoting an agenda, especially a political one. Inclusive leadership in organisations isn't about your political affiliation. It's about embracing diverse perspectives and leveraging them to support workplace goals.

To take a quick account of where you are currently in these approaches, you can take the *Inclusive Leadership Self-Assessment* at www.silewalsh.com/ilnoc-resources

Is Inclusive Leadership Always Good?

The short answer is no, of course not! Nothing is always good, and the Phantasy* or desire for it to be is part of the problems inclusion and inclusive leadership face in organisations.

Besides the obvious issues that the research has spoken to, such as weakened effectiveness with power distance (Guo, Zhu & Zhang, 2020) and poor implementation (Leroy et al., 2021), cultural differences (Ashikali, Groeneveld, & Kuipers, 2020; Yanzi & Yanan, 2019), and the context where it is applied (Agbenyega & Sharma, 2014), one of the main issues with inclusion and inclusive leadership is that leaders can weaponise it to avoid responsibility. It can be misused or weaponised by employees to further their own agenda.

When leaders weaponise it, we see them avoiding responsibility, using inclusive leadership as a way to avoid decisions or centre a decision they want to make anyway but pretend they are serving inclusion.

When employees weaponise it, they try to use inclusion agendas to serve their own personal, relational, or professional goals. They use it to "win" something rather than see that they have a responsibility to others, too.

Additionally, as I previously discussed, it can be misinterpreted as people apply societal expectations to their experience in organisations.

What, How, And Not Just Who!

When I talk about inclusive leadership and inclusion, perhaps because of my background in systems-psychodynamic coaching, I'm not just thinking about who. I'm thinking about what is or isn't being included, as well as how we are doing inclusion. When only related to identity, we miss the subversive way we can limit inclusion while patting ourselves on the back for including those based on identity.

"psychodynamic coaching aims to help clients walk less noisily through the forest of life, understand what triggers them, get below their defenses, and support them in seeing more options. To go beyond the rabbit hole, to see the bigger picture and to join up the dots in their life."

—— Dr Sebastian Green

When we include this broader perspective, we stretch beyond conscious identity and into both the conscious and unconscious aspects of life, which influence how we relate to ourselves and others, in other words how we do inclusion.

If we include these people but not these things, not these thoughts, not these ways of being, not these traditions, then what we are doing is not inclusion. Inclusion needs to be more than who. It needs also to be what and how. When we aren't thinking about what we are including and who we are including, we start to split. We begin to exile parts of the human traits and humanity, cognitive functioning, and all of the inherent complexities of humanity. We start to exile them and reject them.

We need to think about inclusion as who, what, and how we're including –

> » What conversations are we not having?
> » What things are we avoiding?
> » What examples do we not value?
> » What research methods or data are we not including or not valuing?
> » How are we going about it? Are we stopping inclusion before it even starts?

We need to think about inclusive leadership encompassing who, what, and how to function and produce better outcomes. I've often worked with organisations where we co-created strong processes and relationships that led to shared insights that senior leaders were equipped to interpret findings and integrate them to plan actions to support the organisation's purpose and strategic alignment.

However, I've also had cases where my reports didn't end up at the final stage. Every time this happened, it was because the information I gathered was not what a particular group or individual wanted to be communicated to the senior team.

Often, the current reality of inclusion work is that those deemed responsible for implementing it have agendas, sometimes helpful, sometimes not. Additionally, those responsible for implementing it may have additional tensions they have to balance that often unconsciously prevent it from occurring.

This becomes an issue because, in diversity and inclusion work, we are gatekeeping the knowledge unless we are facilitating a shared responsibility and competency related to inclusion by allowing multiple stakeholders to understand it from multiple perspectives. This can keep diversity and inclusion practitioners in the know and, therefore, in power. This can then lead to another issue, which is that it is only the practitioner's lens being thought about and understood.

In cases where this happens, CEOs and C-suite executives may take a directive from their DEI lead that is politically aligned with the DEI lead's position but not helpful to the work of DEI in the organisation. My most recent example is a number of practitioners encouraged senior leaders to comment on political issues that had no link to the organisation's DEI activities, which later resulted in arguments, discrimination cases, and even cases where parts of the organisation came out against the senior executives' public statement to say they disagreed with it—leading to some awkward PR.

We need to ensure that multiple stakeholders can think about and understand multiple perspectives of the conversation, not just the conversation that one particular group or individual in an organisation wants you to have. This affects the how aspect of inclusion in organisations. If we don't allow people to process and mature their insights, then they cannot develop and support the work effectively.

This is so important because if we exclude information, data, and perspectives, then we are not being inclusive. If we are allowing people to have voices but then excluding aspects of the voices that we dislike, without utilising a process that cultivates an informed view, we are likely to keep replicating part of the pattern that may, in fact, be causing issues.

Then, we are not acting in an inclusive way simply by excluding that information and perspective. It's our *how* that is limiting inclusion.

When we do that, we are doing something with the power of our role, and we're doing something with our personal power and how that power is being used. Often, we are replicating the power issues that underlie the limitations to inclusion.

We are talking about inclusion while excluding perspectives, insights, points of view, and data that we disagree with. Inclusion cannot occur unless it also includes the What, Who, and How.   41

In organisations, we talk about inclusion through legislation. But what we include is often another way of managing exclusion. If we do not allow certain conversations to occur, if we do not allow certain points of view to be shared, and if we do not allow certain pieces of data to be considered, then we are acting exclusionary.

It cannot be an individual's agenda. That is not about the organisation's inclusion; it's really about their own beliefs, values, and political positions in the world. This is not inclusion. When we utilise the space in work to discuss inclusion to further our own external political agenda, then we are not fulfilling our role and are misusing our power and responsibility.

The Transformative Power of Inclusive Leadership

The concept of inclusive leadership has emerged as a pivotal factor in driving performance, innovation, and employee well-being. There is much data and empirical evidence supporting the benefits of inclusive leadership and its impact on teams and organisations.

While I do not want this book to be an academic piece of work but rather a practical insight into inclusive leadership in organisations, I think it is important to still share some core benefits to inclusive leadership that we know the research has led us to understand and harness further.

> *"Inclusive leadership fosters an environment where innovation and creativity flourish. Workgroups supported by inclusive leaders are more likely to think outside the box and develop innovative solutions."*
>
> ———————— Bourke & Titus, 2020

There is a whole industry focused on innovation and many different types of MBAs, Masters, and micro-credentials. Yet, in my experience, they rarely consider how inclusive leadership can lead to more creative and innovative outcomes. Instead, they try to squeeze traditional leadership views into the approach. On the other hand, inclusive leadership delivers on innovation so strongly that it is worth focusing on as an innovation approach. Suppose the team supported by inclusive leadership lacks diversity. In that case, there will be constraints on the innovation the team can generate together, inevitably limiting the range of perspectives and problem-solving approaches within the team and restricting the potential breadth of solutions.

> *"Employees working under inclusive leaders report feeling 70% more included, which contributes to a more cohesive and effective work environment."*
>
> ———————— Bourke & Titus, 2020

Let's think about inclusion and inclusive leadership as leadership that facilitates a sense of belonging as well as the ability to value and utilise one's uniqueness. We can see how employees could feel more connected and more aligned. This could develop a more effective way of working than if we compare it to colleagues who don't feel that they belong or don't feel that their unique perspectives are valued. Then, of course, that will automatically have a different felt experience for employees.

> *"Teams led by inclusive leaders are 17% more likely to report high performing, thereby contributing to organisational success."*
>
> — Bourke & Titus, 2019

An often-overlooked benefit of inclusive leadership is improved performance. When people can be themselves without masking or code-switching, they can focus better on tasks, leading to higher performance within teams.

> *"Such teams are also 20% more likely to say they make high-quality decisions, which is crucial for the long-term sustainability of any organisation."*
>
> — Bourke & Titus, 2019

We hear all the time about better decision-making and thinking about higher-quality decisions, but rarely do we pull that apart to understand its components. Let's think about high-quality decisions, which are important in organisational life. We have to consider what types of leaders can influence and impact that experience so that people can make decisions that they feel are of better quality. If we spend our time masking, code-switching, or feeling psychologically unsafe, the quality of our decisions will be impacted. It's quite

44

natural for our defences to kick in and attempt to pre-occupy us with our own safety concerns rather than the quality of the decisions we're making and how they relate to the organisational purpose.

> "Inclusivity promotes collaboration, with teams being 29% more likely to report behaving collaboratively."
> — Bourke & Titus, 2019

Again, collaboration is spoken about quite frequently, as is innovation. Still, we don't always think about how the organisation structures procedures and KPIs and that what is valued may impact collaboration. It's fine to expect people to collaborate. But, if the responsibility falls on one person or the deliverable only belongs to one person, collaboration becomes a tick-box exercise rather than something that results in more effective outcomes. This is why we need to think about inclusive leadership and collaboration through the lens of performance and effectiveness so that we don't allow collaboration or inclusive leadership to become a tick-box exercise or a technical endeavour in which somebody either does or doesn't succeed. Instead, we need to see it as a process in which collaboration is an ongoing activity rather than something assigned to certain meetings, times of day, or relationships.

> "A 10% improvement in inclusion can increase attendance by almost one day a year, reducing the costs associated with absenteeism."
> — Bourke & Titus, 2019

If we feel included, that we matter and belong, then of course, we will not be taking sick days as often as we would in environments where we don't feel we belong or matter and don't feel included. Currently, people are talking about how performance, employee engagement, employee wellness, and inclusive leadership can directly impact those experiences. Instead of always targeting one individual outcome you're trying to achieve, implementing inclusive leadership can lend to several improvements.

> *"Psychologically healthy organisations, often a byproduct of inclusive leadership, experience five times less staff turnover."*
>
> — APA, 2014

Psychological safety, in the context of the workplace, can be defined as teams feeling a shared belief that members feel safe and able to take interpersonal risks, such as speaking up and engaging in voice behaviour (Edmondson, 1999; O'Donovan, McAuliffe, 2020). A team with high psychological safety possesses a high level of mutual respect and trust (Edmondson, 1999; Kolbe et al., 2020), and therefore, they have confidence that speaking up will not result in negative consequences, such as embarrassment or rejection (Kolbe et al., 2020).

Psychologically healthy organisations have been described as workplaces where both employees and the organisation can thrive. This encompasses a workplace that promotes employee's psychological health and well-being and is not just focused on maximising profits. There are generally five elements to a psychologically healthy workplace: employee involvement, work-life balance, health and safety, recognition, development and communication (Grawitch, Gottschalk and Munz, 2006; Gratwich & Ballard, 2016). A psychologically healthy workplace is not an end-state but rather a process to meet the needs of its employees with continuous improvement (Gratwich & Ballard, 2016).

It's really important to know that inclusive leadership can support psychological safety and healthy organisations. Psychologically healthy organisations can support inclusive leadership as it can allow leaders to practise inclusion more effectively. There are so many savings and benefits from supporting a psychologically safe work environment and a psychologically healthy organisation. Things as simple as reduced recruitment costs, reduced sick days, reduced legislative cases, improved retention, and improved employee engagement and loyalty. The list goes on. Inclusive leadership is good for business not because it's a moral standpoint but because it has so many ripple effects that organisations spend billions every year trying to achieve this balance.

Some data on inclusion states that people who are within inclusive teams are eleven times more likely to be highly effective compared to non-inclusive teams and ten times more likely to be innovative, which will encourage driving organisational growth.

More information includes that it is six times more likely to provide excellent customer service, enhancing brand reputation. Employees in such teams are four times more likely to work extra hard, contributing to better work outcomes, and ten times more likely to report high levels of job satisfaction, creating a great work culture. Also, employees are four times less likely to leave their jobs in the next twelve months, reducing recruitment and training costs.

They are also four times less likely to feel that work has a negative or very negative impact on their mental health. Employees in inclusive teams are five times less likely to experience discrimination or harassment, making for a safer workspace and reducing the risk of litigation.

This data from the *Inclusion at Work Index 21/22, Australia*, overwhelmingly supports the transformative power of inclusive leadership. The benefits are multiple, from boosting innovation and employee well-being to enhancing performance and reducing turnover. Organisations that invest in inclusive leadership are not just doing the right thing. They are also doing the smart thing.

CHAPTER 3: INCLUSIVE LEADERSHIP PRACTICES AND PRINCIPLES

When we are talking about inclusive leadership, organisations repeatedly ask me for a formula, a measurement, and a framework. While there are lots of people who have developed all of these things, I have found that they tend to fall short in application. Not because the model or the formula itself is not accurate or effective but because the application of these models, formulas, frameworks, and measurements can be reduced to tick-box exercises. For this reason, I focus primarily on practises and principles as something that we encourage and measure in the workplace.

One of the main reasons for this is that in a workplace, it is appropriate for us to discuss what is considered appropriate communication and behaviour and how we would like the task or the job to be completed. These practices can be reinforced and addressed when not engaged.

Practises go beyond a single behaviour and speak to an ongoing engagement with the behaviour. However, we also need to engage with a set of principles that can support these practices. Specifically, over the last four years, I have seen a pattern of principles supporting organisations and leaders to be more effective through inclusion.

The thirteen inclusive leadership principles have been born out of the frustration I experienced witnessing the reductionist approach to inclusive leadership and what is effective in multiple different organisations in varying geographical locations, implemented by different groups or parties. The thirteen inclusive leadership principles have come from this observation and pattern recognition.

In no way is this an exhaustive list. However, it is a robust list of principles that support inclusive leadership in organisations in a context-specific way. It views inclusive leadership as a social process with relational engagements and personal practice within it. I share these in no particular order, as they often interact with each other in different ways.

Understanding Inclusion and Its Relationship with Performance and Organisational Purpose.

> *"Diversity and inclusion is a competitive advantage that a smart leader would not overlook."*
>
> — Brian Ka Chan

There needs to be a balance of both utilising inclusive practices and fulfilling the purpose of leadership to develop an effective inclusive leadership practice for organisations. We have to consider the relationship inclusion has with performance and the organisation's purpose. If we don't practice inclusive leadership like this, it becomes something else, something not on *task* and something that can be sidelined and deprioritised as other needs emerge.

To be an effective inclusive leader, you need to be effective at utilising inclusion to support organisational performance and help people thrive.

To embody inclusive leadership, leaders need to ensure that they are open, available, and accessible to all of their people (Nembhard & Edmondson, 2006). This obviously adds an additional expectation to leaders from hierarchy settings in which they can often hide behind their role and have others buffer access.

Fostering a supportive environment, such as listening to concerns and willingness to appreciate peoples' voices regarding any ideas, can make employees more engrossed in tasks and, therefore, increase their job performance and satisfaction (Choi et al., 2015; Nguyen et al., 2019).

An inclusive leadership style, as mentioned, is associated with increased job performance through enhancing factors such as employee well-being, person-job fit, innovative behaviour and mutual respect and recognition (Nguyen et al., 2019).

Inclusive Leadership Insight 10: Inclusive leadership needs to be rooted in supporting organisational performance.

Let's hand this over to you for self-reflection and implementation. Ask yourself and write down your answers to the following questions:

» How do I actively demonstrate the link between inclusion and organisational performance in my leadership style?

» What steps can I take to ensure inclusion is woven into the fabric of our organisational purpose?

» How can I better align my leadership practises to both promote inclusion and enhance performance?

Effective Communications

"The single biggest problem in communication is the illusion that it has taken place."

— George Bernard Shaw

We need to consider what effective communication is. This differs from organisation to organisation because there isn't a template or standardisation for effective communication.

However, effective communication is not about what you say or do. It's about what people understand.

Effective communication is based on the impact the communication has on the message that was communicated rather than your preferred way to communicate or what you said.

When coaching senior leaders, they often discuss communications that may not consider whether they are effectively understood, trusted, or misinterpreted, if they're sufficiently communicated, or if there is potential undermining to what was said by other organisational activities.

To be an effective inclusive leader, you need to be an effective communicator. Effective communication is paramount in the realm of inclusive leadership, serving as the bedrock for successful teamwork and enhancing organisational performance. It fosters understanding, trust and collaboration. For communication to be truly inclusive, it needs to be clear, compassionate, and embracing. Ambiguity in messaging can easily lead to misunderstandings, while compassionate communication requires the active consideration of others' perspectives, needs, and feelings from their viewpoint rather than one's own assumptions.

The study titled *Inclusive Leadership and Effective Communication: An Unbreakable Bond* (Jain, N., 2018) underscores the significance of communication skills for inclusive leaders. It argues that such leaders employ these skills to make team members feel included, valued, and listened to, particularly when navigating cultural misunderstandings and differences within a team. This emphasises the critical link between inclusive leadership and effective communication strategies in creating a cohesive and high-performing team environment.

Inclusive Leadership Insight 11: Inclusive leadership needs to connect to what people hear and feel, not what we say.

Let's hand this over to you for self-reflection and implementation. Ask yourself and write down your answers to the following questions:

> » How can I adjust my communication style to ensure clarity and inclusivity for all team members?

» What feedback mechanisms can I implement to understand the impact of my communications?
» How do I promote a culture where effective communication is seen as a shared responsibility?

Leveraging Differences

"It is not our differences that divide us. It is our inability to recognize, accept, and celebrate those differences."

——— Audre Lorde

Diversity is a fact of the human condition. Diversity of identity, experience and points of view is central to all of the fabulous results inclusive leadership can harness when we speak about innovation, creativity, and more.

However, inclusive leaders need to stop seeing diversity as surface-level knowledge about someone and start looking at all the ways they promote sameness. Get the data you need about diversity, correct the things you know are continuing inequality, but focus on the mechanisms for differences to be leveraged.

Based on the work that Short et al. (2011) did around the fact that inclusion needs the balancing of uniqueness with belonging, I think it's essential to know that when we are attempting to leverage differences, they can lead to more robust creative and innovative outcomes than if we continue to engage comfortably within the homogeneous norm.

Suppose you're practising inclusive leadership, or you are attempting to support the organisational purpose but have not created room for differences. In that case, those who are different will find other ways to express themselves and communicate their needs.

You can have an organisation full of diversity and still not be inclusive. In other words, you can have an inclusive organisation that is not diverse. One without the other leaves potential on the table. Inclusion is the practice of creating space for differences to add value. This is something we need to train ourselves to be.

An inclusive leader is only effective when they can facilitate differences and utilise them for task completion.

Inclusive leadership is a multifaceted approach that strives to ensure every member of an organisation feels valued, understood, and leveraged for their unique contributions.

Building on this, a systematic review by Korkmaz et al. (2022) of 107 academic articles on inclusive leadership clarifies the behaviours that constitute inclusive leadership, proposing a model that functions at multiple levels, such as individual, team, and organisational. This model comprises four dimensions that recognise employee uniqueness, enhance team belongingness, show appreciation, and bolster organisational efforts towards inclusion. It stresses the importance of embracing employee uniqueness, where leaders both accommodate and celebrate individuals' diverse needs and creative potentials within teams, akin to transformational leaders who inspire innovation by valuing and encouraging team creativity.

Shahana Banerjee eloquently captures the essence of diversity and inclusion by comparing it to culinary art. Diversity provides the ingredients, while inclusion blends these to create a magnificent dish, highlighting the collective genius that drives innovation and progress. Without inclusion, the potential of diversity remains untapped and unproductive.

Echoing this sentiment, John Graham articulates that inclusion transcends mere representation. It's about valuing and harnessing diverse perspectives to propel organisational success forward. Inclusive leadership nurtures a sense of belonging, making every team member feel valued for their distinct contributions. By genuinely valuing diversity, organisations can unlock a wellspring of creativity and innovation, as a diverse group introduces a variety of perspectives, fostering the development of well-rounded solutions with global relevance.

Together, these insights underline that inclusive leadership is not just about acknowledging diversity but actively engaging with it to foster an environment where every individual can thrive, contribute, and lead to the collective success and innovation of the organisation.

Inclusive Leadership Insight 12: Inclusive leadership is about leveraging differences, not just accepting them or seeking them out.

Let's hand this over to you for self-reflection and implementation. Ask yourself and write down your answers to the following questions:

» What practical steps can I take to ensure differences are not just acknowledged but actively leveraged within my team?
» How can I challenge and change practices that promote sameness over diversity?

» In what ways can I facilitate conversations that explore and value differences?

Utilising Curiosity

> *"The power to question is the basis of all human progress."*
> — Indira Gandhi

In organisations, there's often a pronounced emphasis on expertise, knowledge, and guarantees, privileging certainty over the exploration of the unknown. This preference for knowing over discovering can inadvertently undermine the value of curiosity, learning processes, and adaptability. Ironically, this need to know underscores a broader systemic issue and links to constructs of white supremacy and the management of anxiety. White supremacy, as defined by sources such as Merriam-Webster and Britannica, encompasses beliefs and social, economic, and political systems that uphold white superiority and privilege over other racial groups.

For inclusive leadership to foster new outcomes, enhanced experiences, and deeper engagement, embracing curiosity over certainty emerges as a critical practice. Leaders lacking in curiosity may fail to fully grasp the challenges, needs, and perspectives of those they lead, potentially inflating their ego and overestimating their insight or control. In so doing, they pose a risk to organisational integrity.

Understanding when to leverage curiosity and recognising when anxiety or impatience is taking over is essential for effective inclusive leadership. The importance of curiosity is

57

echoed in both practice and literature. Practically speaking, when a leader demonstrates an open mindset and deep curiosity about others and can engage compassionately without judgement, it is much easier to be effective in the complex, messy work of leadership than if one were to be closed-minded, judgemental, and certain, as the latter is more likely to result in defences of the other and a lack of insight on the leaders part. Research by Thompson and Klotz (2022) supports the notion that leader curiosity enhances psychological safety, encouraging open communication within teams. This study constructs a model illustrating how curiosity positively impacts psychological safety, which in turn facilitates a culture where team members feel safe to express their thoughts and ideas.

The concept of curiosity is pivotal for leaders to navigate uncertainty and foster creativity. As outlined by sources like the *UC Davis* and *Forbes Coaches Council*, curiosity can be dissected into three components: openness, perspective-taking, and coping with ambiguity. Together, these elements equip leaders with the flexibility to creatively adapt to change, drawing parallels to an actor exploring their character. By nurturing curiosity, leaders can cultivate a more inclusive, dynamic, and innovative organisational culture, underlining the transformative power of embracing different ideas and experiences for growth.

Inclusive leadership insight 13: Inclusive leadership is most effective when we use curiosity and co-creation.

Let's hand this over to you for self-reflection and implementation. Ask yourself and write down your answers to the following questions:

» How can I foster a team environment where curiosity is encouraged and valued?
» What practices can I adopt to demonstrate my commitment to exploring over knowing?
» How do I balance operational pressures with the need for curiosity and exploration?

Effective Collaboration

"Alone, we can do so little; together, we can do so much."

—— Helen Keller

Mere collaboration without a clear purpose or strategy does not foster meaningful action or results. True collaboration requires a clear understanding of the objectives at hand and a concerted effort towards how individuals can work cohesively to achieve these goals. In my experience of working with leaders, discussions around collaboration often unconsciously veer into the realms of competition or compromise while they misuse the word collaboration to explain these. However, both of these stances are indicative of underlying power struggles, which are antithetical to the essence of genuine collaboration. When leaders are caught in a cycle of either compromising their needs to avoid conflict or competing to dominate, the potential for productive collaboration is significantly undermined.

Effective collaboration is predicated on the collective focus on desired outcomes and the development of strategies that avoid power struggles, allowing for a synergistic approach to problem-solving. Inclusive leaders excel in this area by sharing power and fostering an environment where collaborative efforts lead to superior results than could be achieved individually.

This perspective is echoed in the field of Organisational Development (OD) and Inclusion. Inclusive leadership highlights *effective collaboration* as a cornerstone, noting that inclusive leaders empower team members, value diverse thinking, and ensure psychological safety, thereby enhancing team cohesion. Similarly, J. Deppeler's work, *Developing Inclusive Practices: Innovation Through Collaboration,* underlines the importance of collaborative innovation in developing inclusive practices.

Further supporting this, research in various sectors, including education and healthcare, demonstrates that inclusive leadership practices that emphasise collaboration contribute to better outcomes. These studies illustrate that when leaders prioritise inclusivity and collaborative efficacy, it leads to enhanced performance and innovation across the board, reinforcing the significance of effective collaboration in achieving comprehensive success in the workplace.

Inclusive leadership insight 14: Inclusive leadership requires collaborative approaches.

Let's hand this over to you for self-reflection and implementation. Ask yourself and write down your answers to the following questions:

» What specific actions can I take to dismantle power struggles and foster true collaboration?

» How can I ensure that collaborative processes are inclusive and engaging for all team members?
» What strategies can I apply to clarify and align team objectives for enhanced collaboration?

Growth Mindset

"Never limit yourself because of others' limited imagination."

— Dr Mae Jemison

Cultivating a growth mindset is immensely beneficial for inclusive leaders, enabling them to perceive challenges, risks and opportunities with a lens that recognises the potential for development and innovation. This mindset fosters the belief that abilities and understanding can be developed through dedication and hard work, which is crucial for leaders aiming to create inclusive environments. Embracing a growth mindset allows leaders to view themselves and their teams as works in progress, nurturing a culture of continuous learning and adaptability. This approach not only fuels curiosity but also reassures leaders that there is always room for growth and development, an insight supported by the NeuroLeadership Institute's research on the significance of a growth mindset in promoting inclusion.

Inclusive leadership insight 15: Inclusive leadership is easier with a growth mindset.

Let's hand this over to you for self-reflection and implementation. Ask yourself and write down your answers to the following questions:

» How can I model a growth mindset to encourage development and innovation within my team?
» What can I do to support my team in viewing challenges as opportunities for growth?
» How do I create a safe space for failure and learning, reinforcing the value of a growth mindset?

Emotional Intelligence

"You may not control all the events that happen to you, but you can decide not to be reduced by them."

— Maya Angelou

Enhancing emotional intelligence (EI) is pivotal for reinforcing inclusive leadership, as it significantly enriches leaders' ability to navigate the complexities of diverse workplaces with insight and empathy. The development of emotional intelligence – the capacity to be aware of, control and express one's emotions and handle interpersonal relationships judiciously and empathetically – equips leaders with the skills needed to be more perceptive and responsive to the needs and feelings of their team members.

This emphasis on emotional intelligence as a cornerstone for inclusive leadership is also supported by scholarly work within the field of Organisational Development (OD) and Inclusion. For instance, Shalabi and Shalabi (2023) underline the critical role of emotional intelligence in leadership, stating it as foundational for grasping the deep significance of embracing diversity in the workplace. Their work in *Global Citizenship and Its Impact on Multiculturalism in the Workplace* illuminates how emotional intelligence lays the groundwork for leaders to understand and leverage workplace diversity effectively.

Furthering this narrative, Dickerson (2022) presents a compelling model illustrating how emotional intelligence underpins effective leadership practices, particularly highlighting how EI competencies, such as social awareness, are crucial for leading with diversity, equity, and inclusion (DEI) skills. Dickerson's research suggests that principals and leaders who demonstrate high levels of emotional intelligence can foster culturally responsive environments that encourage motivation, nurture relationships, and ensure rigorous and relevant teaching and learning practices.

In essence, the cultivation of emotional intelligence among leaders is not merely beneficial but essential for practising inclusive leadership. It allows leaders to approach diversity and inclusion challenges with a more informed, empathetic, and comprehensive perspective, thereby enhancing the overall efficacy of their leadership practices in diverse organisational settings.

Please note in traditional conversations about emotional intelligence and research, the focus is on empathy.

However, in my experience, empathy is limited as it requires one to have an understanding of the other's experience. In terms of diversity, this is not helpful as it can reinforce the idea that how we experience and understand something is how others do. Additionally, what is traditionally known as compassion fatigue is far more likely to be empathy fatigue, as described in *Compassion Does not Fatigue!* by Trisha Dowling. I do not want leaders to be empathetic and, therefore, run down by the emotional weight of their own and others' experiences. I want to encourage leaders to lead with compassion. So, within this book, empathy will be named, as it is what the research speaks to, but know that my nuanced take is that I am encouraging compassion, not empathy.

Inclusive leadership insight 16: Inclusive leadership requires us to develop our emotional intelligence so that we can engage with differences with more ease.

Let's hand this over to you for self-reflection and implementation. Ask yourself and write down your answers to the following questions:

» What steps can I take to enhance my emotional intelligence for more inclusive leadership?
» How can I use emotional intelligence to better connect with and understand my team's diverse perspectives?
» In what ways can I demonstrate empathy and understanding in my daily leadership practices?

Strategic Practices

Approaching organisational work merely as a series of tactical tasks without aligning these efforts with the strategic objectives of the organisation leads to superficial outcomes. This approach often results in ticking boxes, organising sporadic feel-good events, and creating fleeting moments of inclusion that fail to instigate systemic change. Inclusive leadership needs to be woven into the strategic fabric of the organisation, fostering practices that are not only inclusive but also strategically aligned with the organisation's broader goals to cultivate lasting impact.

This perspective on the strategic integration of inclusive leadership is additionally supported by research within the fields of Organisational Development (OD) and Inclusion. Alkheyi et al. (2020) revealed in their study that strategic leadership practices have a significant impact on knowledge sharing and team effectiveness, underscoring the importance of strategic approaches in enhancing organisational performance. Their findings suggest that by adopting strategic leadership practices, leaders can foster an environment conducive to sharing knowledge, which can enhance the effectiveness of their teams.

Similarly, research by Yas et al. (2023) demonstrates the positive effects of strategic leadership styles on employee performance, particularly through the facilitation of information sharing. This study illustrates how strategic approaches adopted by municipal leaders can evidently improve staff performance, highlighting the broader applicability of strategic leadership in various organisational contexts.

Inclusive Leadership Insight 17 echoes the sentiment that true inclusivity in leadership is inherently strategic. It involves utilising inclusive leadership practices in a manner that is deliberately aligned with and supportive of the organisation's strategic aims. By embedding inclusive leadership within the strategic planning and execution processes, leaders can ensure that their efforts contribute to sustainable, systemic change that advances both inclusivity and organisational success.

Inclusive Leadership Insight 17: Inclusive leadership is most effective when we are more strategic through utilising inclusive leadership practices.

Let's hand this over to you for self-reflection and implementation. Ask yourself and write down your answers to the following questions:

» How can I effectively integrate inclusive leadership into our strategic objectives?

» What measures can I implement to ensure that strategic planning embraces diversity and inclusion?

» How do I ensure that our strategic practices not only achieve goals but also foster an inclusive culture?

Effective Use of Power

> *"The most common way people give up their power is by thinking they don't have any."*
>
> — Alice Walker

The nuanced management of power dynamics is critical yet frequently neglected in discussions around inclusive leadership. Leaders need to scrutinise whether their actions contribute to power struggles, oppression, and dominance or whether they are fostering an environment of enablement or submission. Without this reflection, there's a risk that attempts at inclusive leadership will unintentionally echo the very power imbalances they aim to dismantle. True inclusive leadership involves a deliberate practice of empowerment, choosing to engage with one's own power positively and inspire empowerment in others rather than relying solely on traditional sources of power.

This perspective is supported by several voices within Organisational Development (OD) and Inclusion. Davis and Rogers (2023) have contributed to this discourse, arguing that dominance-based power widens the gap between leaders and employees, while mutualistic power expressions can bridge this divide, fostering a culture characterized by low power distance. Their work advocates for a separation of power and hierarchy to cultivate a culture where empowerment is prioritised, emphasising the development of others' power as a key strategy.

"Mastering others is strength. Mastering yourself is true power."

———————————————————— Lao Tzu

Research by Zhao et al. (2023) further clarifies the complex relationship between power dynamics and inclusive leadership, revealing how high power distance can undermine the benefits of inclusive leadership, affecting team proactivity and collective thriving. Conversely, Tapia and Polonskaia (2020) highlight how mismanagement of power can not only disrupt inclusive behaviours but also have detrimental effects on a leader's cognitive processes.

Empowerment as a facet of inclusive leadership is also explored in literature and media, with articles on platforms like Forbes and LinkedIn reinforcing the importance of empowering diverse voices within organisations. Such empowerment is not just about making individuals feel valued but ensuring they feel integral to the team's success, driving innovation and maintaining competitiveness in dynamic markets.

These insights collectively underscore the importance of reevaluating power within the framework of inclusive leadership. By fostering an environment where power is used to empower rather than dominate, leaders can contribute to creating more equitable, thriving, and proactive teams, ultimately advancing the overarching goals of inclusivity and diversity within organisations.

Inclusive Leadership Insight 18: Inclusive leadership requires us to have a relationship with our internal and external power and how we use that power.

Let's hand this over to you for self-reflection and implementation. Ask yourself and write down your answers to the following questions:

» In what ways can I use my power to empower others and champion inclusivity?
» How can I remain vigilant to the ways in which power dynamics impact team dynamics and inclusivity?
» What practices can I introduce to ensure a balanced and equitable distribution of power within my team?

Cultivating a Learning Environment

"Failure is an important part of your growth and developing resilience. Don't be afraid to fail."

—————— Michelle Obama

Inclusion inherently embodies a learning experience, as there is no one-size-fits-all approach to inclusive leadership. This necessitates a willingness to continuously learn and listen, understanding that inclusive leadership is not something done to someone but rather practised alongside others with a focus on certain practices to guide or assess developmental progress.

69

Creating a supportive learning environment and engaging actively in one's learning journey are essential aspects of this process. A significant obstacle to inclusion and leadership development is the misconception that leaders need to be infallible. This unrealistic expectation hinders the growth of inclusive leadership, as true leaders need to embrace learning and release the burden of shame associated with not having all the answers.

The concept of humility, being free from pride or arrogance, is critical in this context and is supported by various sources within Organisational Development (OD), and leadership. Humility is discussed by Randel et al. (2018) as a character trait essential to inclusive leadership. While there needs to be more evidence of this from a practice perspective and hypothetically, I have witnessed the power of humility at play in workplaces.

The importance of leaders being modest about their capabilities, acknowledging mistakes and facilitating contributions from others results in a feeling of inclusion as those behaviours role model belonging and uniqueness towards oneself. Furthermore, the notion that leaders who admit their faults and embrace their limitations are more trustworthy and authentic is echoed in discussions on true inclusive leadership. Such leaders foster collaboration, recognise the value of diverse contributions, and ensure all team members have a voice.

Hendy's (2022) work on the role of intellectual humility in leadership underscores humility as a predictor of well-being, improved team decision-making, resilience, openness to diverse viewpoints, and leadership success. Additionally, Trinh (2019) found that experts with high levels of humility tend to be more adaptable and flexible as their expertise grows, enabling them to meet changing situational demands effectively.

These insights stress the importance of creating a learning environment in inclusive leadership. Leaders need to be humble, embrace ongoing learning, and recognise inclusion as a continuous aspect of personal and professional development.

Inclusive Leadership Insight 19: Inclusive leadership requires us to cultivate a learning environment and be OK with not getting everything right the first time.

Let's hand this over to you for self-reflection and implementation. Ask yourself and write down your answers to the following questions:

» How can I lead by example in creating a culture of continuous learning and humility?

» What initiatives can I introduce to encourage learning from mistakes and embracing unknowns?

» How can I ensure that learning opportunities are accessible and inclusive for all team members?

Navigating Complexity

"The ideal art, the noblest of art: working with the complexities of life, refusing to simplify, to "overcome" doubt."

— Joyce Carol Oates

The emphasis on navigating complexity within this book stems from the observation that inclusion and inclusive leadership are too frequently simplified into technical frameworks. While such frameworks might offer a basic understanding, they fall short of achieving genuine inclusion or improving outcomes. This reductionist approach often leads to mere box-ticking, adherence to political correctness, and evasion of the inherent complexities within an organisation.

True inclusive leadership requires adapting these concepts and challenges to each organisation's unique context, ensuring actions are fitting, timely and appropriate. Inclusive leadership should be integral to addressing an organisation's challenges rather than an afterthought or additional task. It involves delving beyond superficial interpretations of diversity to foster a work culture that truly empowers and includes everyone, regardless of race, ethnicity, gender identity, sexual orientation, age, and so on.

This approach transcends the simplistic ticking of boxes. It's rooted in fairness and equity, prompting leaders to be deeply compassionate about others' experiences. It's not about fulfilling quotas but about transforming attitudes and the overall workplace culture, showing a genuine commitment to equality and equal opportunities. Such leadership acknowledges the complexity of inclusivity and seeks to embed it within the fabric of organisational culture, ensuring that inclusion is not just an exercise in compliance but a cornerstone of organisational excellence and fairness.

Inclusive Leadership Insight 20: Inclusive leadership is most effective when we can engage with complexity rather than rush through it.

Let's hand this over to you for self-reflection and implementation. Ask yourself and write down your answers to the following questions:

» How do I approach the complexities of inclusion in a way that respects and values diverse perspectives?

» What strategies can I employ to prevent oversimplification of diversity and inclusion challenges?

» How can I better incorporate an understanding of complexity into my leadership decisions?

Co-creating Conditions for Performing

> *"Talent wins games, but teamwork and intelligence win championships."*
>
> — Michael Jordan

Co-creating Conditions for Performing (Walsh, 2022) highlights a crucial aspect often overlooked in discussions about performance enhancement, which is the collaborative establishment of favourable conditions for peak performance, extending beyond individuals to encompass the broader scope of environments and organisations. This approach underscores that performance enhancement is a collaborative effort rooted in relational dynamics and the specificity of context, 73 making inclusive leadership inherently relational and contextually sensitive.

Deloitte's research supports this by identifying *confidence and inspiration* as key components of inclusive leadership that co-create optimal conditions for performance, enabling individuals to voice their ideas freely and motivating them to excel.

Dale Rose's insights further illustrate that inclusive leaders not only facilitate the emergence of top talent but also nurture conditions where those who are new, in the early stages of their careers, or undergoing cross-training can contribute meaningfully and grow into future stars. This inclusive approach to talent development ensures a culture where everyone has the opportunity to excel.

Research by Vessal and Partouche Sebban (2021) demonstrates the positive impacts of active co-creation on individual well-being, work performance and team resilience, reinforcing the value of co-creative practices in fostering a productive and supportive work environment.

Inclusive Leadership Insight 21 encapsulates the essence of these discussions, highlighting the necessity for leaders to cultivate the skills and practices of co-creation. By embracing and implementing co-creative strategies, inclusive leaders can effectively support and enhance the performance of individuals and teams, fostering an environment of collective growth and success.

Inclusive Leadership Insight 21: Inclusive leadership needs us to develop the skills and practices of co-creating.

Let's hand this over to you for self-reflection and implementation. Ask yourself and write down your answers to the following questions:

» How can I facilitate a co-creative approach to problem-solving and performance enhancement?
» What steps can I take to ensure that performance conditions are inclusively designed and implemented?
» How do I balance individual and team contributions in the co-creation of performance conditions?

Group and Team Dynamics

"There's nothing wrong with being part of a group. Humans are social, so it's no surprise that people band together. In fact, many important human achievements, like the civil rights movement, are inspired by groups. But group behaviour can also create a sense of division."

— Jessica Speer

Group dynamics are crucial yet frequently overlooked elements of inclusive leadership. This oversight can lead to a failure to address the *how* of inclusive leadership, especially if the nuances of how groups and teams

75

engage, perform, and manage anxiety are ignored. Inclusive leadership is fundamentally about co-creating performance conditions, necessitating a collaborative approach where responsibilities are shared to solve problems and enhance performance. This process is intrinsically relational, emphasising the importance of context-specific actions in fostering an inclusive environment.

Wilfred Bion's work on group dynamics is a foundational theory in the field of group psychology, offering deep insights into the subconscious underpinnings of how groups function. Bion identified several key concepts that explain the often irrational behaviours observed in groups, centring on what he termed *basic assumption groups*. These assumptions are modes of unconscious group activity that members fall into, particularly under stress or uncertainty, which can significantly influence the group's dynamics and effectiveness.

Inclusive Leadership Insight 22: Inclusive leadership is most effective when leaders can engage with the unconscious and not just the conscious efforts of a group.

Let's hand this over to you for self-reflection and implementation. Ask yourself and write down your answers to the following questions:

» How can I better understand and influence the unconscious dynamics that affect group and team performance?

» What practices can I implement to ensure that group dynamics support inclusivity and collaboration?

» How do I address the challenges that arise from group dynamics in a way that strengthens team cohesion and inclusivity?

Why now?

> *"Part of the problem is that we tend to think that equality is about treating everyone the same when it's not. It's about fairness. It's about equity of access."*
>
> —————— Judith Heumann

Workplaces are inherently designed unconsciously for certain norms, which reduce the capacity for everyone to succeed. This means that as the workplace diversifies and markets become ever-increasing, inclusive leadership is needed.

In many countries, discrimination is prohibited by law, but active inclusion is not mandated. Moreover, in some places, discrimination is legally sanctioned.

Examples –

- Inclusive leadership creates more robust outcomes through innovations, profits, employee engagement, and performance. It does all the things organisations are constantly having to manage.
- Our workplaces are changing, and so are the expectations of the workforce. Inclusive leadership ensure you have the competence to engage with people in effective ways without advantaging those like you.

77

- As political polarisation is on the increase, the workplace requires inclusive leadership more than ever. This additionally brings fear up for people, as does the rapid changes that have occurred over the past ten years in Ireland, the UK, and Europe as a whole.
- Effective practice of inclusive leadership can create more robust outcomes, including affecting innovations, profit, employee engagement, performance, employee retention, sick days, and positive brand associations.
- However, the workplace is changing, and so are the expectations of the workforce.
- There is a high narrative around inclusive leadership and inclusion, and we have to consider how the political world is influencing our organisational life and our internal thought processes.

When I work with people, they either share these thoughts or indirectly disclose them. Inclusive leadership means something to everyone. Inclusion brings up numerous different feelings and fears for everyone. Leadership means different things to different people.

This leads to questions and thoughts along the lines of:

- What about me?
- Are we lowering standards?
- Do you mean quotas? If you do, will it be an advantage or disadvantage for me? Are we giving people an unfair advantage?

- How am I disadvantaged? (because it may give me power in a different way now!)
- I'm not the issue – they are. Others need to learn more.
- But I heard a story... prisons, sports, madness.
- "I am better than those who believe that or do this" – moral righteousness.
- What if I get cancelled?
- There is too much focus on minorities and ignoring majorities.
- Can't we just get on with it? I don't know why it is such a big topic.

Each of these examples represents genuine thoughts. However, none of these help with inclusion or inclusive leadership in organisations. Most of the time, we think about inclusion from a social or political perspective, but in this book, we discuss it from an organisational perspective. Nevertheless, politics permeates our organisations, as do individuals grappling with their thoughts, feelings, and inquiries.

Inclusive Leadership Insight 23: Inclusive leadership is not about perfection or selflessness. Instead, it is about a very human relationship with ourselves and others.

CHAPTER 4: ARE WE REALLY DISCUSSING THE SAME THINGS?

Often, when I teach about inclusive leadership, it becomes evident that although we believe we're having a unified discussion, we may be employing identical language with vastly different interpretations. I was reminded recently about how important definitions are whenever I work with organisations, especially around employee resource groups or inclusion committees.

The definition and the differences in understanding can become a big barrier to alignment, cohesion, and effective practices. People often join employee resource groups or inclusion committees with personal agendas for change, which can sometimes distract from the group's main objectives.

Being served implies individuals prioritise their personal agendas over fostering a shared understanding of diversity, equity, inclusion, and belonging, despite the varied interpretations and experiences associated with these concepts.

Inclusive Leadership Insight 24: Inclusive leadership is about moving from me to we.

The meaning of the words we use is important because they signify the way in which we are thinking about something and the way in which we are trying to communicate. There are a couple of definitions I think need to be clarified. It may be helpful to consider the way in which I'm using them so that when you read them, you can understand them from that perspective.

Additionally, it's important to know that some words are thrown around and used as if they mean the same thing or something else. They may have a very different meaning. Therefore, legislation, policies, and day-to-day language communicate a different nuance.

The following are the definitions I prefer to use, and I think they clarify essential aspects of this topic. But like everything, there are many valuable variations you may want to consider yourself. However, in reading this, you need to understand what I mean and not just what I say.

A quick reminder of previously defined terms:

> *"Inclusive leadership in organisations is the effective use of inclusion practices in all forms of leadership to support psychological safety, experiences of inclusion, and organisational performance."*
>
> — Sile Walsh, 2022

Inclusion practices refer to fostering and facilitating
the perception of belonging and uniqueness (Shore

et al., 2011). Additionally, the sense of not belonging doesn't necessarily require deliberate exclusion. Rather, it can arise from subtle cues of one's identity not being compatible (Slepian & Jacoby-Senghor, 2020), such as a sense that this space wasn't designed for me or someone like me. Formal and informal leadership is any form of leadership that influences others within a group (Ehrhart & Naumann, 2004), regardless of the title.

> *"Remember what I told you. If they hated me, they will hate you."*
>
> — Sinead O'Connor

Microaggressions – A behaviour used to further marginalise a member of a marginalised group that is directly reinforcing something that dehumanises or decentres the person and furthers their experience of othering.

Bias – Inclination towards or against something in our thinking, whether conscious or unconscious.

Othering – Positioning people different from you in an oppositional position as the other, and in doing so, furthering a space between your identity and theirs while also inherently attaching a judgement to the othering.

When I speak about isms and phobias – Racism, Sexism, Ageism, Ableism, Classism, and Anti-Semitism – The *ism* implies structural or societal reinforcement.

Homophobia, Transphobia, Xenophobia, Islamophobia, Atheophobia, and Fatphobia are interesting terminology, as *phobia* implies fear and, in this context, points strongly to social processes in which in and out groups form, rejecting those perceived as the *other*.

83

Isms, in this context, usually imply a structural or societal reinforcement. For instance, every race can be discriminated against. However, racism requires structural reinforcement, so only some instances are racism, and others are discrimination.

Calling in – An invitation to raise awareness about bias, prejudice, microaggressions, or discrimination to aid an individual's learning.

Calling out – Drawing public attention to negative language or actions as a means of making a public statement (Harvard University).

Marginalisation – Treating a person or group as less than, as other, or as less important.

Oppression – The use of power over individuals and groups, most commonly through systemic means in which one person or group norms or preferences are given power over another.

Please note: Different countries have different laws about which groups are protected under discrimination or equality law. However, the social act of micro-aggressions, oppression, bias, and discrimination may go beyond the legal definition of a particular country at a particular time.

Intersectionality – Intersectionality is a theoretical framework for understanding how aspects of a person's social and political identities (gender, race, class, sexuality, ability, etc.) combine to create different modes of discrimination and privilege. The term was coined by Kimberlé Crenshaw in 1989 to describe the compounded experiences of bias and disadvantage that occur when multiple intersecting factors contribute to social inequality. Intersectionality highlights the importance of considering the overlapping and interdependent systems of discrimination or disadvantage that cannot be examined by looking at singular aspects of identity in isolation.

Management versus leadership – While there is much debate over this, I use a simplistic definition. A manager's work is strongly aligned with operational work, whereas leaders are working with more strategic elements of organisational life. Leaders need followers, whether through direct reports or through their influence in thinking or social influence. Managers keep the organisation going by ensuring the day-to-day realities are met and that their management is about maintaining something. A leader is about going somewhere.

Microaggressions

Some examples of microaggressions include:

☐ Acting as if someone is inferior due to their gender, race, or sexual orientation.

☐ Drawing conclusions about someone based on their religion, age, or social class without evidence or explanation.

☐ Intentionally choosing not to use the preferred pronouns of a transgender individual due to their transitioning process.

☐ Failing to adequately portray various races, sexualities, and disabilities in media.

☐ Refusing to acknowledge the offensiveness of sports team names that are stereotypical or derogatory.

☐ Using derogatory language, such as "That's so gay."

☐ Believing that individuals of certain ethnicities, social classes, or sexual orientations are superior to others.

(Medical News Today, 2022)

Microaggressions can be done by anyone to anyone. However, in inclusion work, the focus is usually on systemic oppression when considering microaggressions. This is because microaggressions are often invisible to most people who aren't part of the targeted group, often built on unconscious beliefs and commonly are unintentional but still harmful.

Bias

Bias is a natural cognitive process that streamlines our thinking and enables us to navigate the world around us quickly. Our brains are wired to engage in this unconscious, rapid decision-making as a protective measure against potential threats.

Although biases are an inherent aspect of human cognition, they can pose challenges in the context of inclusion. In many cases, biases have become embedded within systemic ways of viewing the world and can lead to the dehumanisation or undervaluation of certain individuals or groups. This can ultimately limit the effectiveness and robustness of decision-making processes.

Inclusive leadership seeks to address these biases by recognising their potential impact on our ability to relate to and collaborate with others. By acknowledging that biases serve as a protective function while also understanding their potential limitations, we can work to develop more evolved ways of engaging with one another and making informed decisions.

It is important to note that biases are typically automatic and unconscious, making them difficult to identify and address without intentional effort. By actively seeking to understand how biases can limit our perspectives and decision-making processes, we can work toward a more inclusive and equitable society.

Bias is the inclination or prejudice for or against one person or group, especially in a way considered to be unfair. (Oxford Dictionary)

Types of Bias include Affinity bias, Confirmation bias, Gender bias, Name bias, Beauty bias, Halo effect, Horns effect, and Conformity bias.

Prejudice constitutes a preconceived belief devoid of reason or genuine experience, falling within the broader category of bias. It encompasses various forms, such as racism, sexism, ageism, ableism, classism, antisemitism, homophobia, transphobia, xenophobia, Islamophobia, atheophobia, and fatphobia.

Bias Interrupters can be really helpful from an organisational perspective. It is an evidence-based model that provides solutions. It disrupts the constant transmission of bias in basic business systems, which leads to more diverse and better-performing workplaces. Bias Interrupters change systems, not people. (Bias Interrupters, 2023)

Discrimination

One aspect of workplaces that demands our attention is when we suggest that people should be *authentic* and *bring their whole selves to work.*

While we want to encourage authenticity, the idea of encouraging employees to bring their whole selves to work is somewhat counterintuitive as it's not exactly true. The reality is we don't want people to explicitly engage their authentic selves as this can complicate and contradict what we want to occur in the workplace. For instance, what do we do when a person participates in racist or discriminatory beliefs, does something illegal, or has beliefs that may become difficult in the workplace when we have encouraged them to bring their whole selves to work?

Off-the-cuff statements such as these ignore the psychological perspective of authenticity, which most scholars would agree is an ongoing discovery of self and that there isn't a stagnant authentic self that exists within any one person.

Additionally, when we suggest a person should bring their authentic self to work, we're quite frankly being naive and impractical. We can be in alignment with ourselves without bringing our authentic selves to work.

When we enter the workplace, our primary aim is to contribute to the tasks at hand. While it's important to create an environment where people don't feel the need to mask, code-switch, or conceal aspects of themselves due to discrimination fears, this doesn't equate to genuine authenticity.

But also, we aren't clarifying that the bottom line in a workplace is always to be your appropriate self yourself appropriately as long as it doesn't contradict the purpose of your work, is not considered to facilitate discrimination, and doesn't prevent you from contributing to work.

We are affirming that you shouldn't need to expend energy concealing your identity as we're committed to preventing discrimination. Nevertheless, it's crucial that everyone actively contributes to the organisation and tasks at hand. If expressing your authentic self impedes effective communication, behaviour, or task completion, we cannot endorse that either.

Inclusion isn't the direct opposite of discrimination. The opposite of discrimination is non-discrimination. The opposite of inclusion is exclusion. However, it's possible to be in a workplace where discrimination doesn't occur yet and still not feel included.

Equally, it's important to remember that inclusion is an invitation, but it's an invitation that we need to all offer to each other. No single person can be held responsible for it. The balance of uniqueness and belonging needs to have boundaries in organisations, with the purpose of the organisation being a primary driver along with the legislative responsibilities that are in place. There needs to be some clear boundaries about what we do and don't do in the workplace. This isn't to prevent inclusion but to express and be explicit about expectations.

Another aspect to consider is when you don't have explicit expectations. What can happen is that implicit ones come in, and they are often not agreed upon and can be rooted in unconscious, oppressive norms from historical systemic norms. So, when something is expressed, we have the opportunity to challenge it. We can discuss it and ensure it serves the purpose it's meant to serve.

When it is implicit, we can't do that because we have to name it, and then we have to process whether people agree that it exists and whether our interpretation is correct or not. At the same time, explicit statements are the boundaries that we need to lean into.

We need to consider what happens when two characteristics or groups protected by discrimination law conflict in the workplace.

Leaning very heavily on Myra Khan's work about two truths, we can start thinking about the difference between being included and prioritised over others.

There is a difference between being dehumanised and not being understood. When we talk about being authentic or bringing your whole self to work, what we're talking about is that people don't spend their time needing to mask, code-switch, or manage the systemic implicit implications that come with historic systems norms that are oppressive.

It is not oppression because we dislike it. It is not discrimination because we don't like it. It is only discrimination when based on the current legislative interpretation of who is protected by discrimination legislation and is treated less favourably based on this interpretation. It is only discrimination when the characteristics protected under the law are being treated less than. Inclusion, authenticity, diversity, and differences are complex issues and challenges in the workplace. They continue to be an ongoing challenge because we don't always address the underlying reason for the challenges. Instead, we address the situation that emerges. The core issues often stem from normalising the marginalisation and devaluation of certain individuals, which becomes embedded in systems, benefitting some while creating barriers for others.

If a situation emerges that is related to diversity, equity, and inclusion, there are probably gaps in the structures, processes, and practices that could be improved. If they're improved, you can not only deal with this situation more effectively, but you can prevent it from occurring and moving forward.

It's appropriate to learn some of these things as we go. We can't know everything in advance, especially because inclusion is an ongoing, evolving, and emerging context. Instead of trying to do all these things, what we need to do instead is have ways to handle them that invite progress in some way.

When we are thinking about inclusion, we need it to be embedded as a business-as-usual activity. We need inclusion to be how we solve problems as opposed to a separate additional problem to solve.

Inclusive Leadership Insight 25: Inclusive leadership is about solving problems with inclusive leadership practices.

Inclusion means that we need to be explicit about the boundaries and expectations, behaviours, and ways of communicating what we expect in the workplace. Inclusion doesn't mean that everyone is happy and gets everything they want.

What Is and Isn't Inclusive Leadership?

There are many misconceptions as to what inclusion and inclusive leadership are. These misconceptions become challenges to implementing inclusion practices and inclusive leadership in organisations. A couple of the common ones that frustrate me are this notion that if I'm using the right language or being nice in a politically correct way, I am being inclusive. It couldn't be further from the truth. You could use the right language, and it could be politically correct while still excluding.

Understanding the latest language or labels and specific group needs doesn't equate to advancement in inclusion. It just reflects awareness of certain differences.

Sometimes, the desire to get inclusion and inclusive leadership right leads to this phantasy about never making mistakes and a fear that if I make a mistake, I'll be invalid or I will have shame. Inclusive leadership, because it's an ongoing practice, is something that will involve mistakes. We will need to be able to apologise, to be able to learn and regulate during these moments when we may feel shame or a desire to reject ourselves or be challenged.

Inclusive Leadership Insight 26: Inclusive leadership is not about getting everything right. It's about practising inclusive leadership and moving towards more inclusive experiences.

Another common belief about leadership is that it is a senior leadership responsibility for inclusion. The reality is, as we defined in the beginning, inclusive leadership isn't simply a positional leadership approach. It is also related to those who engage with thought leadership and social leadership. Your senior leaders are not in every room or every conversation, and while yes, they can role model and lead the way, it is not the senior leadership's sole responsibility to develop an inclusive, high-performing organisation. That is a collective task in every organisation.

Inclusive Leadership Insight 27: Inclusive leadership is a form of distributed leadership, and everyone has a different responsibility.

Sometimes, when I'm working with human resources or people or culture teams, they desire to do the right thing and tick the box for inclusive practices. However, in reality, that is the very opposite of inclusion.

You can do some tick-box exercises for aspects of diversity because you are measuring something *that is*. But, when it comes to inclusion, it is about reinforcing a process and a practice that enhances inclusive leadership and inclusion in the organisation. What can be helpful is to view inclusive leadership in a similar way that we engage with health and safety efforts.

It's an ongoing important practice that makes everything better but isn't necessarily natural or built into how we've already learned to do things (this recommendation and analogy was made by a participant in one of the first inclusive leadership pilot programs I ran, and I think it's one of the best analogies to date).

As discussed previously, inclusion is not the opposite of rejection. So, let's not think that rejection or the opposite of rejection is inclusion because it is quite normal for people to believe that their intention of inclusion is the same as the impact that they're having. That isn't accurate. While we have to measure the impact and outcome of inclusive leadership because it's far more complex, it is important to note that what we're looking for is the benefits of inclusive leadership in your organisation. An element of measuring is assessing the impact you're having, but you cannot measure your success based on impact alone.

Inclusion is making decisions to discuss issues as they arise related to diversity, equity, and inclusion:

- ✓ It is about supporting and encouraging employees.
- ✓ It is about practising active listening and utilising open questions while actually listening for answers that might be different to your preferred ones.
- ✓ It is about consistent, clear communication all round and not just top-down.
- ✓ It is about focusing on strengths and the differences people bring and how they can add value to the task at hand.
- ✓ It is about accepting responsibility appropriately and doing better.
- ✓ It's about following up with less active staff and asking for their contribution and preferred ways of engaging in meetings.
- ✓ It is about consciously connecting with people who are not the same as you, regardless of your identity and whether you or they are marginalised or not.
- ✓ It's about catching your own assumptions about others and watching for any biases that might be limiting your ability to be inclusive.
- ✓ It's about attempting to co-create psychologically safe working environments and to normalise a learning environment.
- ✓ It is about self-educating when you learn that there's an area that you're lacking in.
- ✓ It's about ensuring that you are up to date on what might be considered a microaggression

towards people or if an unconscious bias might be affecting those you work with.

✓ It's about actively hiring from a wide variety of backgrounds.

✓ It's about praising efforts more than criticising.

✓ It's about being considerate of scheduling so that you're considering personal lives, work hours, religious needs, care needs, and community needs.

✓ It's about assessing the pay structure and compensation to look for any inequity across your pay structures.

✓ It is about support and cross-departmental relationships, providing a safe place for employees to feel valued and heard.

✓ It's about creating a system and processes that allow you to address misunderstandings and resolve disagreements in an effective and timely manner.

Inclusive Leadership Insight 28: Inclusive leadership is an activity, not a conclusion.

Oppressive Inclusion

Often, what is missed in discussions about inclusion and equality in the workplace is actually an understanding of the inherent assumptions that begin with inequality.

For instance, white supremacy finds a way to integrate itself into organisations quite easily, as does classism and ableism. While you may have a different experience of these depending on your own identity and positionality, there's also an understanding of what these terms mean and how they might present in the workplace.

I'm not here to give a lecture or provide lessons on white supremacy or classism. However, I do want to discuss how these issues manifest in the workplace, highlighting how things we may overlook can perpetuate classism, white supremacy, or ableism.

The three aspects of classism, white supremacy, and ableism overlap. I'm not using racism directly but rather focusing on the normalised system that upholds these issues. I'm talking about classism because that's the easiest terminology to use to talk about the system in which class impacts your equality of opportunities.

The big tenet of white supremacy is, in fact, perfectionism, and this is something that also plays out in classism. The Centre for Community Organisation's research has shown that the requirement for *perfect* work in organisations is often applied unequally on the basis of race. For example, racialised employees are held to a higher standard, while white employees are allowed to experiment, mess up, learn, and improve. *Mistakes* by racialised employees are seen as representative of their value as staff members overall and even of their racial group. In contrast, white employees are given the *benefit of the doubt*. Their research has also documented a pattern where racialised employees are punished for things that would not even qualify as mistakes or are being held accountable for expectations that were never made clear to them. A common occurrence is when a racially marginalised employee is assumed to spearhead diversity or anti-racism efforts in the organisation without it being specified in their job role. They are then blamed for the failures or conflicts that arise from those initiatives or their lack thereof.

I've noticed certain recurring patterns when collaborating and working with individuals from various socioeconomic backgrounds across Ireland, the UK, and broader Europe.

One of the main reoccurring issues is how imperfection and humaneness are dealt with. Another is how, in workplaces, when people are dehumanised or required to be less of themselves, the roots of white supremacy, ableism, and classism can be found within those conversations.

I express this without pointing fingers or assigning blame. I say this to acknowledge that systems privilege some things over others, and that's quite a normal experience. The issue is that when a system normalises privileging one thing over another, it also then normalises devaluing the other. When we talk about white supremacy, ableism, or classism, it means devaluing people who fall lower on the white supremacy value, the classist value system, or the ableist value system.

When we think about white supremacy, some of this will be in terms of fat phobia and body weight. Some of this will be related to pretty privilege, and some will be related to clothing modesty and what is deemed as beautiful, acceptable, important, and privileged. These are some ways that it can show up because we know that within certain professions, industries, and organisations, how you dress matters.

I still hear women, more than anyone else, speak about how difficult it is to dress in the workplace. Underneath all of the systems and isms of oppression is a prevalent occurrence that we deem some as good and some of lesser status. No matter how decisions are made about who meets the standard and who doesn't, sustaining any form of oppression requires additional oppression. This is where that intersectional lens becomes important, and it's also where we need to think about what we are normalising in our workplaces, what we are saying we expect versus what is actually occurring. These women are often never told what they need to wear. Yet, time and time again, they are able to tell me what is expected of them dress-wise and what would happen if they didn't adhere to the unofficial dress code. Often, they have experiences where they had to come in on a day off or wear comfortable shoes, resulting in changing the way they usually dress. This left them feeling uncomfortable in the way they were treated.

In workplaces, we simply replicate what happens in society, and we need to acknowledge that before we can have conversations about zero-tolerance policy.

In any type of zero-tolerance policy regarding unacceptable behaviour, we first have to acknowledge that we've normalised much of the behaviour in society. This will, of course, enter into our organisations because organisations exist within society.

Society is made up of people, organisations, networks, groups, laws, legislation, and so many other things. So, it's really important to know how your workplace may continue to replicate perfectionism, sexism, racism, classism, ableism, etc. Not because you intentionally go out of your way to do it but because they exist and are inherent in society, and we replicate them in organisations.

The majority of readers here likely reside in countries with discrimination laws in place. This implies that within your organisation, there's an expectation to refrain from discrimination based on the legislation applicable. So, while it might be inherent in society because of how power is traded, shared, and struggled over, it doesn't mean that it is acceptable or appropriate in the workplace or that it should continue. That is why legislation is in place.

However, taking it a step further, people who are othered, who are not treated as equal and who have to put in extra effort just to be accepted are less likely to thrive at work. You are less likely to get the most out of them in your workplace. You are less likely to have a workplace full of psychological safety and difficult conversations that result in better understanding and more practical solutions to inclusion.

Without such considerations, we risk resorting to checkbox approaches. Identity-focused decision-making may aim to avoid discrimination risks without truly confronting systemic oppression patterns. I invite you to find ways that you can practice inclusion in an intersectional way so that every group and every identity can inform you about what they need in order to thrive at work without being reduced to a label.

An intersectional approach to inclusive leadership embraces the unique backgrounds, experiences, thoughts, and perspectives of each individual. (Praslova, 2022; Thompson, 2024)

In Ireland, we have a term around disabilities, which is *reasonable accommodations*. I would argue in many cases, the reasonable accommodations are quite reasonable and maybe aren't being met. However, in other cases, I would argue that some requested accommodations aren't reasonable for the workplace. We need to prioritise creating broader accessibility and recognise how individual solutions can benefit many. Let's move beyond minimum standards and embrace the advantages of reasonable accommodations, enabling everyone to thrive and contribute effectively in the workplace.

Inclusive Leadership Insight 28: Inclusive leadership can be more effective when an intersectional lens is utilised.

Splitting and Shame

Níl saoi gan locht – There's not a wise man without fault.

———————————————— An Irish Saying

To talk about inclusion and inclusive leadership honestly, we have to acknowledge that there is a lot of splitting and shame that occurs. To be inclusive of another is to be inclusive of the parts of ourselves that we reject, the phantasies of how organisations should be and also how other people should be—working with the reality of what is here and now without ignoring the future that we can create or the history that now has been built upon. Often, without discussing inclusive leadership, inclusion involves meeting oneself and each other with more compassion and a desire to learn and understand rather than with certainties or guarantees. And, of course, this can be confronting because shame exists within that context, and shame is very often not spoken about in the context of organisations. Nor are the phantasies of a perfect organisation, team, manager, or leader. Consequently, the combination of these factors leaves us feeling deeply frustrated with the current reality or in denial about it. If we cannot confront the shame that arises when we need to acknowledge our less-than-ideal qualities, then we will remain in a stalemate.

One of the main questions that come up, time and time again, is, "How do I let people know that they are being racist, homophobic, exclusionary, or discriminatory?" The reason this is so challenging is that we have associated all of these isms and phobias with being a bad person.

We have located the issue within the individual. When we do this, we provoke the individual's shame, meaning they have to reject it, deny that they are these things, or justify it. We do this instead of locating it within the system and acknowledging that societies are inherently full of isms, phobias, biases, and discrimination, and that is quite a normal but undesired factor of society.

Therefore, it should be acknowledged as a normal expectation to be confronted by within an organisation. Normal means that it is a default, the lowest and easiest common denominator in terms of behaviour from human beings. We need to recognise that as long as we keep placing the blame on individuals and use language that triggers individual psychological defences, we will keep dealing with shame whenever we discuss inclusion and inclusive leadership.

What I'd like us to do during this journey is to think about inclusion as a conscious intention. If we do this, we can humanise the process of inclusion rather than replicate the oppression of others. If we continue to facilitate shame and splitting in ourselves and others, we are simply using the same tools of oppression. As Audrey Lorde says, "You cannot take down the Masters House with the tools that built it." (Lorde, 1984) I invite you to understand that shame is directly related to inclusion and that the ideas and phantasies we have about inclusion might also be part of the issue we have.

Inclusive Leadership Insight 29: Inclusive leadership can trigger shame, splitting, and phantasies or be supported by compassion.

CHAPTER 5: WHAT DO WE NEED TO CONSIDER TO BE MORE EFFECTIVE?

When I asked one of my brothers what quote gives him hope and inspiration, he shared this with me –

Safety is not the absence of threat but the presence of connection

———— Gabor Matte

As we engage in the work of inclusive leadership, we often encounter several common challenges that can hinder our progress. Through my years of experience in leadership development, coaching, and the application of inclusion in promoting psychological safety, improved engagement, and higher performance, I have identified several recurring obstacles. These challenges include but are not limited to individual psychological defences, group dynamics and defences, misconceptions about the nature of inclusive leadership and a pervasive sense of overwhelm.

In the following pages, we will explore these challenges in more detail, providing you with considerations intended to support you in overcoming them. I encourage you to use these resources when you encounter challenges.

Some of the challenges that arise in organisations, which I have seen as barriers to their efforts, are listed below. Shifting these can massively impact your efforts and ensure that your inclusive leadership efforts lead to effective leadership.

These challenges can include:

When we do not align our efforts to overall business purpose and prioritises, we will not be successful. To create sustainable and effective inclusion practices, ensure they align with organisational strategy.

When we engage in inclusion in an oppressive way, we will lose people. Do I want people to believe in inclusion? Yes. But do people change when forced to consider something I believe in? No! Furthermore, by itself, it lacks inclusivity.

If we do not acknowledge that change brings fear and that inclusion means sharing power, people will often struggle with that shift because it feels threatening. We have to work with this fear and not try to push it away, avoid it, or deny it, as it will continue to fester and find inconvenient ways to express itself.

Viewing organisational inclusion through a societal and political lens rather than an organisational lens is limiting. This leads to so many misconceptions that people end up disappointed and misaligning the remit of organisational inclusion.

Challenges arise when we treat inclusion as an additional and parallel practice rather than integrate it into business-as-usual activities. We need to incorporate it; otherwise, it will be deemed more work and deprioritised as other priorities more closely related to the business need attention.

DEI/EDI practitioners own the process rather than supporting others to own the process. This is a tough one, as when your KPIs are directly related to the work and others aren't, it can easily result in a misplacement of responsibility. Like leaders, HR professionals can't be in every room and conversation. They can set systems up and support development, but everyone in the organisation is responsible and needs to be.

DEI, EDI, HR practitioners and diversity experts promote their personal political views rather than stay closely aligned with the role of DEI in organisational performance. We need to know that there are professional boundaries between our activism and our role in an organisation. When this is blurred, the fallout is very messy.

When there are no boundaries to inclusive leadership, it becomes an unachievable expectation of keeping everyone happy. We need inclusive leadership to be about critical thinking, weighing up options, and engaging people to inform ideas, thoughts, and decisions. However, the decision is still often up to the leader.

Another challenge is collapsing inclusion and discrimination. You can be in a workplace and not be discriminated against while also not being included. For Example, Peri works in a tech company, and Peri is invited to all the meetings and team days. Peri's second language is English, which the organisation supports in multiple ways. Peri is disabled and has all the reasonable accommodations required in the workplace and, therefore, is not discriminated against. However, Peri is not invited to lunch with his colleagues because they assume he wouldn't like to attend their lunch break as it is in a building outside the organisation that is not accessible.

To avoid discrimination and promote inclusion, there needs to be a clear connection to the organisation's purpose, relevant legislation, the values we utilise in our work and what we will and will not accept in terms of communication, behaviour and how someone completes their task. This includes expectations in a code of conduct, KPIs intertwined with standards and not just deliverables. It includes job descriptions integrating communication principles and behaviour examples, as well as clear instructions on how we do the work and which values and ethos we use in our decision-making, with an ongoing process of accountability alongside each of these for all people.

This isn't to prevent inclusion but to define and express it and be explicit about expectations. Inclusion doesn't mean everyone is happy, gets everything they want, and is liked. Inclusive leadership is using inclusion to effectively lead, which inevitably will mean doing things others disagree with.

Language

Language complicates inclusion, as do societal norms and historical meanings. One way to manage this is to discuss diversity and to do so through the lens of oppression rather than identity. An example is discussing racialised people, people discriminated against, or marginalised people.

Discuss what is causing the oppression rather than labelling the group's identity. Many individuals within groups do not resonate with different popular terminology. While a lot of language policing goes on outside these communities, we can find that even within communities that experience marginalisation, there isn't a consensus on language.

If you don't know how to reference someone's identity and it is relevant, ask, "What terms do you prefer to use to describe your experience of race/ethnicity/gender/sex/disability/sexuality/background, etc.?"

If you find yourself wondering if what you said is or isn't acceptable, then it's worth exploring it yourself or with an appropriate person at a later date and correcting it.

I repeatedly use *appropriate* because we often expect marginalised communities to educate us about their experiences, which can burden them with extra labour. I learned this the hard way when George Floyd's murder happened. I texted a friend and asked, "What can I do? I am shocked." She graciously replied, "Why are you asking me?" I was asking her because I thought she lived in the USA.

But I know at least five people in the USA, so the real reason was this – she is a Black woman. We had talked about race, and when reaching out, I wanted to show her I cared and wanted to know what to do. I wanted her to know I was a good person. I also wanted a simple answer from someone with lived experience. The point is, I reduced her at that moment to being a racial advisor, a role she hadn't ever agreed to. Rather than a friend, a role that she had not agreed to. I was also being lazy. I wanted to avoid the discomfort I felt. I wanted to be on the right side of history. The better response was to feel the feelings, observe those publicly speaking about it, and choose to take up the role of educator and engage in my own time to learn.

Language is constantly evolving. When we think about language, we need to consider it a social process, not a stagnant truth.

Additionally, language, by itself, isn't the issue. It is how that language interacts with power and oppression. This is one reason why many marginalised groups reclaim their language, distinct from how those outside the shared identity of the marginalised group might use it. Language is an action that interacts with power, and inclusive leadership is all about using your power to be effective as a leader with inclusive practices.

Inclusive Leadership Insight 30: Inclusive leadership requires the insight that language is always changing and never stagnant.

Agency and Role

When discussing leadership, we often do so from the perspective of recognising leaders' power and privilege. However, we seldom consider the limitations imposed on their agency and decision-making by their roles within an organisation. Each position brings privilege and the responsibility to fulfil the role within the wider organisational system and effectively lead those they work with. Leaders often operate within the confines of their organisation, tasked with achieving specific outcomes within a larger system. Yet, what is frequently overlooked is how these roles sometimes demand actions that may not align with the individual's personal preferences but are required for overall organisational functioning and success.

I regularly encounter leaders aspiring to be effective and ethical. Yet, as they move to higher levels of authority, they often find their roles very different from their initial perceptions. This discrepancy is not merely about the ability to make decisions. It also involves a shift in how they previously viewed their role versus the reality of fulfilling it, which requires additional considerations that impact their agency. While increased power at a senior level is anticipated, the accompanying shift in agency—where actions and viewpoints are perceived as those of the organisation rather than personal stances—is less considered.

Discussions on power and privilege in leadership roles seldom address the implicit or explicit agreement to act in the organisation's best interest and not merely personal or departmental preferences. This adjustment can be significant, as many view leadership through the lens of positional power, overlooking the constraints on those roles in terms of agency. Such constraints are vital. Without fulfilling their role effectively, leaders can create gaps in the organisational system, leading to unintended negative consequences.

This complexity is often overlooked. While leaders can indeed impact through their decisions, they also need to navigate the limitations of their role within the organisation, balancing positional power with the realities of their agency. With positional power comes a responsibility that impacts one's agency—a nuance critical to understanding leadership in organisations and navigating the complexity of organisational life.

Motivations at Work

For many individuals, work is intrinsically linked to their sense of purpose, aspirations, identity, and self-worth, extending beyond salary, titles, or organisational objectives. This presents a nuanced challenge for leaders, as it underscores the need to acknowledge the diverse motivations that drive individuals, thereby influencing their performance and support requirements. For instance, some people may be motivated more by the nature of their work than by financial rewards, dedicating themselves to fields like social work or research out of genuine passion rather than any real connection or alignment with organisational aims. This situation illuminates the complex interplay between intrinsic and extrinsic motivational factors, highlighting how we are all motivated differently and value distinct aspects of our lives and work.

A misunderstanding of these motivations can lead to misguided attempts at staff retention, such as offering higher salaries when an employee might instead value flexible working conditions, the opportunity to work from home, increased public exposure, enhanced learning opportunities, and more. Often, motivations can transcend financial incentives, dispelling the myth that salary is the sole driver of employee engagement and retention. This understanding is supported by economist Dan Pink, who posits that motivation is multifaceted and not driven solely by financial rewards. Indeed, he

suggests that an over-reliance on salary as a motivator

can lead to less effective work outcomes in certain circumstances.

Grasping the breadth and diversity of motivations is essential for navigating organisational dynamics and avoiding the creation of silos. As leaders, connecting individual motivations with the organisation's broader goals is helpful, enabling everyone to see how their contributions integrate into the wider vision. While I encourage this, I know it is no small feat for leaders.

The diversity of motivations enriches organisations and breathes life into them in various ways, yet it poses a challenge that leaders need to navigate adeptly. Dr Tony Humphreys' book, *Work and Worth*, provides an excellent resource for exploring our relationship with work, leading to deeper insights into the motivations of others.

There are myriad reasons why individuals may feel unable to leave a job, even if it offers inadequate remuneration or lacks fulfilment. Such circumstances often exacerbate the challenges faced by those already experiencing marginalisation. Constraints like geographical location, limited opportunities, or financial responsibilities mean that the option to simply leave a job is not available to everyone. This stark reality underscores the need to recognise workplace inequalities that can further impact individuals' motivations and their ability to perform to their potential.

In Ireland, for example, university professionals might face a dearth of alternative opportunities in their area. At the same time, in the UK, government employees could encounter difficulties transitioning between departments or promotional opportunities due to geographical constraints or the availability of such roles.

Some individuals may be in roles that, despite being unsatisfactory, are financially critical due to familial dependents, caregiving duties, or workplace agreements. The decision to change jobs is significant, and the complexities of organisational life necessitate acknowledging that people can feel trapped in unwelcome positions.

Leaders may also find themselves navigating the difficult waters of managing team members who are responding to these realities. This facet of organisational life can introduce a range of frustrations and challenges for all involved. Through the application of inclusive leadership principles, it is hoped that we can navigate these complexities with increased understanding and, consequently, greater success. Acknowledging these challenges is fundamental in our efforts to create more inclusive and supportive workplace environments, as these realities, when left unaddressed, can lead to greater frustration and a stalemate in work teams and relationships.

Intergenerational Shifts

We still tend to generalise intergenerational differences. Often, the assumption is that something is wrong with the other generation. It is one of the biggest generalisations that is still normalised in workplaces and discussed openly. We have a new level of complexity in organisations now, as previously, age and seniority tended to align. However, we are finding less of this alignment with the ever-evolving workplace and different required skills, as well as people engaging in their second and third careers. This leads to all sorts of differences at play, including generational perspectives that were once considered the norm. These ideas are reinforced by peers as they would traditionally have occupied similar positions professionally and personally and are now more visible as the workplace and seniority tends to have more intergenerational differences. Therefore, these values can no longer be assumed to be automatic.

Intergenerational workplaces will continue to grow, and this difference can bring even more richness into the workplace. However, to navigate that well, we need to work with our generational judgements and assumptions to navigate the complexity within our organisations with greater effectiveness and ease. Again, it's no small feat.

The Complexity of Readiness

When discussing inclusion and inclusive leadership, we are essentially addressing the need for culture change, both directly and indirectly. Yet, we don't always contemplate the mechanisms that facilitate such change alongside evaluating the readiness for change. Creating a more inclusive, high-performing, and psychologically safe organisation requires understanding that readiness varies depending on the specific area of focus—be it inclusion, psychological safety, or performance enhancement.

A fundamental part of coaching psychology and organisational development efforts revolves around assessing readiness for change and then nurturing this readiness. Culture change is often perceived as requiring grand gestures or significant events because the aim is to influence the entire organisation. However, when we consider culture change from the perspective of individual leaders, it becomes clearer that change is enacted through the behaviours we endorse or reject, the forms of communication we respond to or ignore, the priority we assign to different types of interactions and people and the decisions we make that influence what structures enable whether it be inclusion or defaulting.

In addressing organisational cultural change, it is crucial to consider the readiness of those involved. I find it particularly useful to view those most resistant to change not as obstacles but as communicators of vital information about the organisation and possible risks. Seeing resistance as a form of communication opens up the possibility of addressing unmet needs and discerning whether the resistance stems from personal issues or highlights broader concerns that can be leveraged to support the organisation's progress.

Embracing this approach allows us to engage with all members of an organisation compassionately and pragmatically. If I reject the individual and their resistance, it is very unlikely that anything can change as we hold opposing positions. Instead, it's about working with what is presenting as it is in the hope of working more effectively with the resistance and the person. This compassionate and practical stance enables us to work with what is without adding to it and furthering the frustration. If we see all expressions of resistance as data, we can unpack that data with less emotional entanglement and more pragmatic approaches.

Control and Frustration

Many individuals I converse with tend to recoil at the mention of control and power, primarily because these terms are frequently associated with negative connotations in their experiences. However, within organisational contexts, levels of control do exist, and understanding how to relate to these levels is crucial for empowerment and influence. A common phenomenon I've observed is the tendency to blame those in higher positions or with more control (I call this the "blame up phenomenon"), often critiquing and judging their decisions. This manifests as blaming those above us, or even those around us, rather than sitting with uncomfortable feelings related to the reality of the situation.

A humorous meme about organisational changes highlights this dilemma. Many raise their hands when asked if they desire change, yet when asked who is willing to change themselves, the room falls silent. This underscores the importance of focusing on what is within our control rather than expending energy on aspects beyond our influence or criticising the actions of others.

Exploring what lies within our circle of control and considering how we might constructively influence outcomes is a far more fruitful endeavour. In this context, influence does not imply coercing others to conform to our wishes—which would equate to control—but rather presenting ideas or actions that might sway their decisions. True influence acknowledges the autonomy of others, recognising that they, too, consider various factors in their decision-making processes.

Shifting our focus to what we can control and how we can positively influence our surroundings conserves energy and fosters a more proactive and empowering approach to organisational life. By concentrating on our capacity to effect change within our immediate sphere, we can contribute more effectively to the collective effort of organisational improvement, steering clear of the unproductive cycle of blame and critique roundabout. However, to do so is to effectively work with our emotions of frustration, grief, and disappointment so that we can then work with what is rather than what we wish it were.

This means that we need to navigate our own feelings, others' feelings, our power and expectations, our realities, and our individual and group defences. The blame and critique roundabout results in further disempowerment and usually more stuckness. Again, it doesn't mean you will like what others do, but the pre-occupation with others in the workplace rarely leads to an unsatisfying experience.

All behaviour is Information

One of the challenges in developing inclusive leadership is such a strong desire for a particular environment that we can dismiss data that feels contrary, challenging, or slow. It is deeply helpful to consider all behaviour as data and to bring curiosity to that behaviour.

> » What unmet need may this be commuting?
> » What has occurred to this person engaging in this behaviour?
> » What could I learn from this situation to equip me with more effective ways of working with them?

» How am I reacting to the situation, and is it enabling it?

These considerations pop us right back into the co-creator position on the empowerment triangle and prevent us from getting stuck in the drama triangle.

We can also apply this consideration to previous diversity and inclusion attempts. It's important to know that much of what I critique within this book is not to criticise the doers of those actions but the actions in and of themselves as ineffective. It is not to say someone is wrong but to say we could improve things. It is not to put down previous attempts, as without them, I could not have formed these observations, insights, and positions. Everything is data, and when we treat it this way, we can work with it more effectively.

Organisations are complex ecosystems, and much of what has motivated inclusion has had to interact with these complex interplays. Much ineffective leadership and management are directly related to the organisational complexities and not simply due to individuals, as are many of the conflictive interactions in organisational change. If we can locate our discussions, insights, and issues within the knowledge of this complexity, we are more likely to find effective solutions than if we over-simplify or reduce a situation to an individual or a single problem. If it were not a complex problem, then the first attempt to solve it would have been successful, and all examples of replicating that process would also be possible. That is often not the case for any leadership or inclusion efforts.

Artificial Intelligence

With the increasing pace of artificial intelligence, we will need to be aware of how AI can assist inclusion and equally limit it. This is going to be an ongoing practice. To promote inclusive leadership, it can be helpful to ask questions about AI efforts in your organisation related to the following, as there is great evidence as to how AI can support and limit inclusion.

- » Does AI in any way bias some people over others? Is this problematic in our organisation?
- » Has this been assessed against a set of inclusion criteria?
- » Can this AI assist our inclusion efforts or inbuild inclusion into its default?

Ways of Working

As hybrid working, work from home, and flexible working are increasing in popularity and expectations, it is important to consider how your stance privileges or limits inclusion. There are multiple challenges with each of these; however, there are also multiple benefits. This conversation isn't going anywhere. While we all have individual preferences, I highly encourage you to consider how these ways of working impact inclusion in your organisation and how they relate to your organisational purpose.

External Political Landscape

It is becoming increasingly important to recognise that the external political landscape has become increasingly global, which means that influences from all over the world may influence how your people experience the world and position themselves. In 2024, as I write this work, the organisations I work with are navigating this more now than ever, resulting in inclusion conversations becoming political ideology debates. While your workplace has a clear purpose, it is and will be influenced by external political agendas. We will be navigating this for a while, and your work as an inclusive leader includes acknowledging that tension without getting lost in it. It is about considering what is appropriate for the workplace and what inclusion looks like regardless of political agendas.

PART 3:
ENGINEERING INCLUSIVE STRUCTURES

> *"If you want to go fast, go alone; if you want to go far, go together."*
>
> — African Proverb

To engineer inclusive structure in organisations, we need to know what is needed, what is a finishing, and what is a first fix. Although all the aspects interrelate, we need to understand how to structure inclusion, not just promote it.

I have often assumed people who work in EDI are going to be more inclusive than those who don't, and I have found that can often be untrue. Additionally, like many, I also assumed those with experiences of marginalisation would be more inclusive than those without. Again, this is not always true because it can be easy to be inclusive of people like us, but it can be a completely different situation to be inclusive of all.

It's easy to discuss inclusion to promote it. It's another to practice it.

> *Irshad showed us that we need to view each person as a complex individual made up of many different facets, both good and bad. If we judge people and label them, we will almost always be wrong. If we connect with others instead of remaining closed off to people with whom we do not agree, then through mutual respect and the exchange of ideas, individuals will become more just and inclusive. And when individuals are more just and inclusive, our society will follow.*
>
> — Alex Brosowsky

CHAPTER 6: WHAT ARE INCLUSIVE LEADERSHIP PRACTICES?

Defining Inclusive leadership more robustly:

> *"Inclusive leadership is the effective use of inclusion in all forms of leadership throughout an organisation with the purpose of co-creating an inclusive, psychologically safe, high-performing organisation."*
>
> — Sile Walsh, 2022

We need to consider inclusive leadership through the lens of effective leadership. Otherwise, it's easy to be distracted by inclusion and not see how it serves the work you do as a leader.

Additionally, effective inclusive leadership involves:

✓ Ensuring adequate opportunities exist for differing views, perspectives, and experiences to contribute to the task at hand. (Randel et al., 2018)

✓ Ensuring there are formal and informal routes for inclusion needs to be met, utilising Wilson's 2023 paper, *The Inclusion Needs of All People*.

✓ Sharing power and responsibility for work and task outcomes in formal and informal leadership positions.

✓ Ensuring that a sense of belonging is co-created on an ongoing basis and is viewed as the responsibility of all.

✓ Ensuring that psychological safety is positioned as a shared responsibility and actively co-created (Bushe, Most of the Advice About Psychological Safety at Work Isn't Helpful, White Paper).

✓ Actively developing leadership capacity for cognitive complexity, pro-diversity beliefs, and humility as recommended by Randel et al. (2018 paper)

✓ Seeing inclusive leadership as an ongoing practice rather than an outcome.

✓ Aligning inclusive leadership with better performance, outcomes and effectiveness based on evidence rather than societal or moral preferences.

✓ Starting with the reality of now, me, and us, rather than the phantasy (M. Klein) of what should be.

✓ Considering systemic influences in challenges and decisions including personal, professional, industrial, societal, organisational, group, etc.

✓ Avoiding overly personalising issues onto self or others and seeing the interplay between individuals and systems.

✓ Taking others' frames of reference into account and not simply centring your frame of reference.

✓ Viewing challenges and criticisms through the lens of requests and unmet needs.

✓ Consider your inclusive leadership through the lens of being, doing, and knowing (Anderson & Ackerman-Anderson, 2001).

✓ Fostering a learning environment where emergent needs and insights are valued rather than used against people for being unaware earlier.

✓ Taking a *strengths* approach to your work, team, peers, and leadership.

✓ Perceiving my role as support rather than control and offering employees autonomy, independence, and adequate resources for their work (Carmeli et al., 2010; Hollander, 2009).

What Does Inclusive Leadership Look Like in Practice?

✓ Leading by sharing common goals and aspirations.

✓ Inviting people to formal and informal interactions.

✓ Supporting different points of view without privileging one over the other.

✓ Using organisational purpose, values, and vision to inform decisions.

✓ Focusing on behaviour, communication, and the task at hand instead of shared values, ideas, and beliefs.

127

✓ Understanding that people do their best work in different ways.
✓ Appreciating that differences add value.
✓ Striving to empower others to thrive according to their individual needs.
✓ Taking feedback on and addressing behaviour.
✓ Raising your awareness of your own *norms* and assumptions.
✓ Inviting people to contribute in ways they feel comfortable.

What inclusive leadership isn't –

☐ Being nice or PC. We can be all these things and still not be facilitating belonging or valuing uniqueness.
☐ Knowing everything about diversity labels and needs. This leads to less listening, more stereo-typing, and a fear of mistakes.
☐ Never making a mistake. Mistakes are part of inclusion and inclusive leadership. It is the skill of repairing that we need to develop.
☐ Senior leadership's sole responsibility is that everyone's responsibility is to facilitate inclusion and inclusive leadership, whether privileged or marginalised, senior or junior.
☐ Tick box exercise (as it can be more harmful – avoid this rather than doing it).
☐ Just a variant of servant leadership or other leadership approaches.
☐ Just the opposite of rejection.
☐ An intention to be inclusive. It's an impact of inclusion that results in benefits.

Barriers and facilitators to Inclusive Leadership

Barriers	Facilitators
Not aligning it with the overall business purpose.	Aligning it with the overall business purpose.
Doing it as an additional and parallel practice to business as usual.	Integrating it into business-as-usual activities.
It is being taught/ developed oppressively, ignoring the complexity.	Developing inclusive leadership as an evolving set of practices or principles instead of rules.
Not managing fear of change, losing power, not being relevant, and failure.	Addressing fear of change, losing power, not being relevant and failure.
Viewing it through a societal, political lens rather than an organisational lens.	Viewing inclusive leadership as a leadership approach to organisational performance.
Focusing on a moral, values or beliefs perspective.	Focusing on behaviour, communication, and task performance.
Thinking we are inclusive.	Knowing we all have a role in being inclusive and being included.
Assuming our intent is the same as our impact.	Listening to the impact of our actions on others, considering our role in the scenario and adjusting accordingly.

Challenges in Organisation:

When we have zero-tolerance policies for any isms, phobias, discrimination, microaggressions, etc., then it often means we don't have any repairing, calling in, or normalising of the process needed to be inclusive. This creates fear, often more for the person on the receiving end than for the perpetrator because it leaves the person to weigh up what you mean by zero-tolerance policy.

This notion, while well intended, ignores that we have inbuilt isms, phobias, discrimination, microaggressions, etc., in society that we all inherit and integrate into our frame of reference.

It ignores the reality that isms, phobias, discrimination, microaggressions, etc., will show up in our workplaces on a spectrum of expressions from extreme to mild.

We need a method to address the spectrum of these issues in the workplace. Otherwise, we don't address it at all and avoid it, or people are let go as the only other option. Two options aren't enough to change the culture of an organisation. It also pushes lesser incidents into the shadows, as people don't want to be seen as *the problem*, and while they want it to stop, they may not feel that their colleague being fired is the solution either.

Getting it wrong isn't the issue; not working to fix it is.

No one can get it right all the time. It isn't humanly possible, as isms, phobias, discrimination, microaggressions, etc., are inherited in all social structures by all people. Every one of us has unconscious and conscious isms, phobias, discrimination, microaggressions, etc. The issue occurs when we act on them without taking responsibility for their impact and when we don't evolve in our social interactions and improve our internal frame of reference based on new insights and understandings of self and others.

It is far more effective to use a traffic light system that has clearly defined behaviours and consequences for the behaviour and support for the person on the receiving end of the behaviour. In some organisations, it's a traffic light system. In others, they frame it as a code of conduct, and in others, it's addressed through mentoring or performance improvement plans. Either way, it is more effective than a well-intentioned, impossible-to-implement zero-tolerance policy. Now, for any of this to work, it means that regardless of hierarchy, anyone can call this out and anyone can be held accountable. Additionally, if others witness it or hear of it and do not enact the traffic light system, they, too, can be held accountable for enabling it.

Inclusive Leadership Insight 31: Inclusive leadership is about dealing with today's reality, not about denying it.

Psychological Defences

Despite our best intentions to be inclusive, we all possess individual defence mechanisms that safeguard our sense of safety and identity. While participating in inclusion work, it is important to recognise that these defences may hinder our ability to consider how our own identities shape our perceptions of others.

Our individual defences can be triggered when we feel threatened, which can, at times, be linked to a

131

lack of knowledge in a particular area or potential exposure or judgment, which can pose challenges to inclusion efforts. Developing self-awareness and emotional intelligence can aid in navigating these defences and working through uncomfortable moments to facilitate greater inclusivity.

Therefore, it is imperative to raise awareness and cultivate skills to manage psychological defences and effectively participate in inclusion work. Doing so will allow us to overcome such challenges and build more inclusive environments.

One of the ways I encourage people to do this is to start from the assumption that we are biased and have internalised forms of oppression that we perpetrate. We should accept this as a default and not as a measure of our moral goodness. This way, when we face an example of this, we can compassionately own it, integrate the learning, and create a change in behaviour.

I generally don't support unconscious bias training due to inconsistent evidence and some problematic underlying assumptions, such as the assumption that knowing something results in doing something differently, which anyone who attended a nutrient class or works in public health can attest to the gap in knowing and doing. Another underlying assumption is that telling people what they think is wrong is going to stop them from thinking that. While the intention is good, it is far too closely aligned with oppressive and harmful mechanisms of change that, if being used against inclusion, would be highly rejected. Additionally, mandating changes in thinking is an oppressive act unless individuals choose to participate willingly and desire the training. I do appreciate that these are often well-intentioned and can feel like a safer way to approach these things, but ultimately, the assumptions underlying them are not well considered, and the results vary greatly from harmful to not harmful and from helpful to not helpful.

However, I do encourage having clear standards around communication, behaviour, and how people do the work—socialising these standards across all people within an organisation and in every role. This targets the point at which unconscious bias manifests itself in organisations. This is the point at which inclusion does or doesn't happen, and this is the point at which discrimination does or doesn't happen.

I promote a curiosity around being aware of when a bias is informing decisions. This can work by being reflective and asking yourself, "What assumptions did I make?" and also noticing when new information surprises you, as often it can be in a blind spot.

Inclusive Leadership Insight 32: Inclusive leadership requires an ongoing relationship with defences, our own and others and striving to move through them rather than get stuck in them.

Group Dynamics

Similar to individual defences, groups can become preoccupied with anxiety and focus on basic assumption groups, according to Bion's work in the 1940s with groups. This phenomenon often arises in group-related work, and my own work has demonstrated that it can especially become relevant in the context of inclusion initiatives.

Me-ness (Bain et al., 1996) refers to a group dynamic in which individuals are preoccupied with their personal agendas rather than the group's shared purpose.

Then there is *we-ness* (Turquet, 1974), which can result in members speaking as though the group has one shared identity, as if there is only one feeling and thought for the whole group, often referred to as the *royal we*.

Pairing is a group's tendency to rely on a specific duo to oversee the group's well-being, while dependency similarly involves relying on a single individual.

Fight, flight, or freeze responses can also occur within groups. In such cases, group behaviour may manifest as unnecessary fighting, avoidance or freezing.

Here's a closer look at Bion's original three:

Dependency: The group operates under the basic assumption that a powerful leader or external entity will solve their problems and meet their needs. Members may exhibit passive behaviour, looking to the leader for guidance, direction, and protection. This reliance on authority figures can hinder the group's initiative and creativity, as members abdicate responsibility for their actions and decisions.

Fight-Flight: Groups operating under this assumption perceive threats either from within or outside the group. In the fight mode, energy is directed towards combating the perceived enemy, which can lead to internal conflict if the *enemy* is seen as part of the group itself. In the flight mode, the group seeks to avoid the perceived threat, either by physically fleeing or by psychologically disengaging from the situation. This dynamic can lead to scapegoating, polarisation, and an inability to address internal issues constructively.

Pairing: In the pairing group, members hold a collective, unconscious belief that salvation will come through the union of two individuals within the group (not necessarily in a romantic sense) who will produce a *messiah* or a creative solution to the group's predicaments. This assumption fosters a state of hopeful anticipation but can also lead to inaction as the group waits for a transformative event or figure to emerge.

Bion's analysis reveals that these basic assumption modes can significantly detract from the group's task-oriented activities, as energy is diverted into fulfilling these unconscious needs rather than focusing on the group's explicit goals. Understanding and recognising these dynamics can be crucial for leaders and members of groups in navigating and mitigating the challenges they pose. Effective leadership, in this context, involves fostering an environment where the group can move beyond these basic assumptions to engage in more rational, task-focused activities. This requires creating a culture of trust, open communication, and shared responsibility, where the group is encouraged to confront and work through its anxieties and conflicts in constructive ways.

An interesting phenomenon around inclusion in organisations is that often inclusion is associated with ideas of being happy with *what I've got and what I want* in the situation, people doing what I think is correct, and people including me.

Often, what can occur is the weaponisation of inclusion because it can be picked up and attempted to be used against an organisation or against people with different identities.

This implies that if you're focused on inclusion and recognise an underserved group within your organisation, making adjustments could create a fairer environment and enhance the overall organisational experience. What can happen then is people can attempt to hijack that because they are used to their own needs being centred. They could also attempt to hijack that because they have some political agenda with the situation, and they want something different from what you're working on.

When we think about organisations, we have to consider the purpose of inclusion and how it is not a *catch-all phrase* that means everyone gets everything they want or that everyone who has an unmet need can have that need prioritised.

This means devising a strategy tailored to the organisation's culture and needs to help individuals overcome barriers, fostering equitable engagement and thriving in the workplace. Now, as I have said already, this can also trigger people to think *what about me,* and that's a term I've heard used on social media. "Whataboutry" can try to hijack that effort because they are focused on themselves, which is reasonable, but they are also concerned with how resources are being allocated. This is important in organisations because when people are in organisations, ultimately, we go to organisations to earn money.

Organisations are expected to provide resources, but challenges emerge when external factors like political agendas come into play. This can lead to the weaponisation of inclusion efforts by individuals with preferred approaches or power dynamics favouring domination.

The irony is this isn't based on identity. None of us are immune to doing this. We can belong to a marginalised group or not, and your relationship with power may be to use power in order to dominate others. We need to think about inclusion very carefully and have boundaries around it when we bring it to life and organisations.

We also need to consider the decision-making process that we are using in our inclusion efforts so that we can target the areas where we can find inclusion has the biggest opportunity, i.e., the biggest gap. We can then support the organisation's strategic agenda. But that doesn't mean we're going to keep everyone happy because lots of people have conscious and unconscious desires, hopes, and expectations of the workplace. That in itself doesn't mean we don't listen to people, and we shouldn't consider things. But it does mean that we can't assume that all input is considering inclusion in the organisation from a *What About Us* shared space. It is more likely that people are thinking about how this will affect them and deciding whether that's what they want or don't want.

It's also important to acknowledge that within every inclusion effort within an organisation, you are still dealing with people who have their own personalities, defences, worldviews, values, beliefs, and approaches. If your idea of inclusion is harmony, then you are unlikely to be developing inclusion, and instead, you're likely to be developing groupthink.

Inclusive Leadership Insight 33: Inclusive leadership is about doing what can be done to improve things rather than doing everything or anything perfectly.

Inclusion as a Process and Practice

Inclusion is a term that is often associated with an end result. However, the concept of inclusion goes beyond just achieving a desired outcome. Inclusion is a practice, something we actively do, and a process that involves continuous growth and development. When we think of inclusion in terms of groups and organisations, there is a deeper level of involvement beyond individual practices. It requires prioritising inclusion, acknowledging and addressing discomfort, and navigating the challenges that come with growth and change. In this way, inclusion is not just a destination but an ongoing journey that requires ongoing attention and effort.

Inclusion is both an individual practice and a group and organisational process, and it's important to understand that both require commitment and discomfort.

At the individual level, inclusion is a practice that requires a conscious effort to be aware of our own biases, beliefs, and attitudes toward others who are different from us. It involves actively seeking to learn and understand the experiences and perspectives of others and intentionally taking steps to create a welcoming and inclusive environment for all.

At the group and organisational level, inclusion is a process that goes beyond individual practice. It involves the collective effort of everyone in the group or organisation to create a culture that values and prioritises inclusion. This requires a commitment to systemic change, policies and practices that promote equity and inclusion, as well as the ongoing evaluation of progress toward these goals.

Understanding that inclusion is a journey allows us to effectively engage with it at a personal, group, and organisational level in a way that is effective, letting us meet it where we are in any given setting.

Inclusive Leadership Insight 34: Inclusive Leadership is an ongoing journey, not something to achieve but something to do.

Overwhelm

Inclusion is a complex concept that requires us to move away from simplistic and technical thinking. However, it is common for people to become overwhelmed when they begin to understand the importance of inclusion and inclusive leadership, often focusing on whether the desired outcomes are achievable. This feeling of overwhelm can lead to avoidance of inclusive practices in their entirety. We need to remember that inclusive leadership is practical and requires us to focus on the next best step at the moment rather than trying to address everything at once or becoming distracted by things outside of our control.

The feeling of being overwhelmed arises when we are unable to handle what is in front of us. Instead, we may find it more effective to try to take a broader perspective while also breaking down changes into smaller, incremental steps that we can take ourselves or with our teams. By using inclusion as a process and practise, we can improve outcomes and add value rather than just seeing it as a binary *yes or no* proposition. This can lead to improved processes and practices, greater robustness, and greater innovation and creativity.

When in doubt, you can bring an inclusion lens into all decision-making, causing subtle shifts and awareness. You don't need to be a crusader or saviour; you simply need to try to elevate decisions, behaviour, communication, and work completion when possible.

Non-inclusive Behaviours

Non-inclusive behaviours will differ based on context, people, organisational culture, geographical culture, professions, and industries, to name a few. Here are some practical ideas, not rules but suggestions, to reflect on.

Some of the following examples may give you something to consider:

☐ Using words, gestures, and other acts or omissions that offend once you are aware.

☐ Making fun of people related to stereotypes, identity, protected categories, or topics that would be undermining.

☐ Micromanaging people.

☐ Being dismissive or disinterested when others are communicating.

☐ Encouraging or enabling destructive behaviours of others.

☐ Misusing power in relationships.

☐ Right fighting or dominating others.

☐ Blaming and shaming others.

☐ Creating division, not cohesion, overtly or covertly.

☐ Not valuing other people's time, experience, or values.

☐ Playing favourites and fostering relationships with people like you.

☐ Stealing others' ideas or work and not adequately referencing their contribution.

- ☐ Harassment or bullying.
- ☐ Verbal abuse, including talking down to, swearing at, name-calling, or aggressively interacting with others at work.
- ☐ Unfiltered comments or jokes that others are hurt or feel uncomfortable with.
- ☐ Indirect communication, such as going around people, using in-jokes, and passive-aggressive behaviours.
- ☐ Excluding or ignoring people at work and any stonewalling of any kind resulting in an experience of exclusion, whether intended or not.
- ☐ Inconsiderate scheduling.
- ☐ Being a bystander to abusive behaviour.

CHAPTER 7: WHAT INCLUSIVE LEADERSHIP TOOLS AND FRAMEWORKS HAVE REAL-WORLD IMPACTS?

Inclusion Strategies

I am often asked for ideas about how we can be more inclusive in our day-to-day interactions and the practical ways to apply these. The five most common suggestions I make are detailed below. They appear to be the simplest to implement since they don't demand extra effort, just a minor shift in approach to typical workplace interactions.

1. Listen first, speak second.

Spend time listening to what matters to people, what concerns them and what motivates them. What are people trying to achieve? Use this understanding to inform how you work and relate to people. This allows people to take up space, centre their needs for a moment, and feel important. Listening to an employee's concerns, motivations, and what they are trying to achieve helps leaders understand their needs and builds stronger relationships. This can help create a sense of belonging among employees, promoting more engagement and performance.

2. Ask Questions, the right ones.
Ask people what they are doing, what is on their mind and what they need help with. When we ask these questions, we give people a chance to tell us about themselves, their needs, and their preoccupations. This can help employees feel more comfortable sharing their thoughts and ideas, leading to increased creativity and innovation.

3. Support yourself and others.
When we aren't supported, we lose the capacity to have compassion and relate to those with different experiences. Offer support, but also feel free to coach your people on what support they need to give themselves, ask for and offer. Growing your capacity, your people, and your organisation in relation to support will dramatically increase engagement, relationships, and team effectiveness.

4. Actively engage differences.
Actively seek different experiences, insights, data, beliefs, and opinions. Don't look for agreement in any setting. Invite different opinions and increase the robustness of your conversations.

Actively engaging in differences and seeking out different experiences, insights, and opinions helps create more robust conversations and solutions. This approach promotes diversity of thought and leads to more effective problem-solving.

5.   *Value uniqueness.*

Find moments and opportunities to value differences, not just seek them, and acknowledge how unique contributions, even if drastically different, increase the quality of the task at hand. This lets people know they and their uniqueness are not only welcomed but are also a team strength.

Valuing uniqueness and recognising and acknowledging the unique contributions of individuals creates a sense of belonging and fosters a culture of inclusivity. This approach can lead to increased employee engagement, satisfaction, and retention.

FARR Model

The FARR model is most relevant when someone accuses you, provides feedback, or disagrees with someone else's perspective or lived experience, which differs from your own.

As an example, one of many scenarios FARR works well with the following:

Alexandra: "I found that joke you told earlier in the meeting quite offensive. It seemed a bit sexist to me."

Jordan: "Really? That wasn't my intention at all. It was just a joke. I think you're being too sensitive."

Alexandra: "But it perpetuates harmful stereotypes. It's not about sensitivity. It's about being respectful and inclusive."

Jordan: "I don't see how. None of the women here seemed to have a problem with it. Maybe you're misunderstanding the humour?"

Alexandra: "It's not about misunderstanding. It's important to acknowledge how such comments can contribute to a hostile environment."

Jordan: "I think you're blowing this out of proportion. No one else complained. Why should I change my behaviour because one person is uncomfortable?"

Alexandra: "It's not just about one person. It's about creating a space where everyone feels respected."

Jordan: "Well, I don't see it that way. I think you're making a big deal out of nothing. It's impossible to say anything these days without someone getting offended."

I started using the FARR model because conversations often stalled when someone brought up discomfort or discrimination, especially if others lacked firsthand experience. This led to disagreements and placed the burden on the person raising the issue to justify their perspective.

As demonstrated in the conversation above, this issue arises so often in day-to-day interactions in organisations. I turned to the models I use in my coaching psychology practice to consider supportive ways people can navigate these with more insight and effectiveness without having to be a diversity expert.

FARR is a combination of mentalisation theory and non-violent communication. It is explained in an acronym.

F – Feel your feelings, acknowledge them, and regulate yourself.

A – Acknowledge and accept their experience as valid and as theirs.

R – Reflect on their perspective with someone who won't enable you. Research the perspective and inform your behaviour moving forward.

R – Repair when possible if harm has occurred. Repair the dynamic with the other person.

Feelings and Responses:

When people are accused of bias, prejudice, or microaggressions, they tend to –

 » Feel fear, shame, anger, confusion, defensiveness, or guilt.
 » Respond by denying, collapsing, defending, overexplaining, rejecting.
 » Act defensively and argue, avoid, agree, freeze, and allow others to agree with their own point of view.

An Alternative Response:

Feel your feelings, acknowledge them to yourself and regulate them. Without being able to move through your own feelings, it can be really hard to understand the other person. First and foremost, your ability to regulate and feel your feelings without acting on them is crucial.

Acknowledge and accept their experience as theirs and valid. Even if you disagree, to argue at this point is to enter into a power struggle, whereas this is about repair and understanding.

147

"Thanks for that perspective. I need to digest that."

"Okay, I didn't realise that had an impact on you."

"I haven't seen it that way before. Let that sit with me."

"That's a perspective I haven't considered."

"That wasn't my intention, but I can understand how that was the impact. I am sorry. "

Reflect on their perspective with someone who won't enable you, research the perspective and inform your behaviour moving forward. Consider that there was a gift in what they shared regardless of the tone or your feelings. Seek to learn in some way from it.

Repair when possible and repair the dynamic with the other person. It takes courage and risk to talk about these things.

In fact, sometimes it can be appropriate to get curious and ask them why. However, sometimes that is not appropriate, as it is shifting the responsibility to them to educate us.

If we applied FARR to the examples above

Alexandra: "I found that joke you told earlier in the meeting quite offensive. It seemed a bit sexist to me."

Jordan: "Did you?" (Feeling really awkward and confused but regulating.)

Alexandra: "Yeah, it perpetuates harmful stereotypes. It's not about sensitivity. It's about being respectful and inclusive."

Jordan: "Oh, OK. I hadn't thought of it like that. I was trying to be funny, but I obviously wasn't. I am sorry I had that impact. I am going to need to reflect on this a bit deeper. Thanks for sharing your experience with me, and I'm sorry about that."

Alexandra: "Yeah, these things are very frustrating."

Jordan: "Yeah, I would say it is. I really will reflect on this."

Alexandra: "It's about creating a space where everyone feels respected."

Jordan: "Yeah, I get that. Thanks for sharing that perspective. I hadn't considered it."

Jordan then goes and reflects, and if the relationship is appropriate, might follow up with another apology and the steps they took to learn about the citation further.

Inclusive Leadership Insight 35: Inclusive leadership is easier when we can move through relationship ruptures with more ease and get better at relational repairing.

Being, Knowing, Doing

Consider your inclusive leadership through the lens of being, doing, and knowing (Anderson & Ackerman-Anderson, 2001).

The concept of inclusive leadership can be better understood by examining its three interrelated dimensions – being, doing, and knowing, as proposed by Anderson and Ackerman-Anderson (2001). While leadership is often perceived solely through the lens of action or behaviour, true alignment and effectiveness in leadership can be achieved when individuals reflect on how they are experiencing each moment emotionally, mentally, and physically (being), the actions they take behaviourally (doing) and the knowledge they acquire (knowing).

149

By adopting this wider perspective, leaders can reflect on their own inclusive leadership, evaluate their strengths, and evaluate their areas for improvement. This reflection involves an assessment of their knowledge, behaviour and felt experiences, allowing for greater alignment between their being, doing and knowing. Additionally, such introspection enables leaders to identify any areas of knowledge, behaviours, or experiences that they may be avoiding, providing an opportunity for growth and development.

Inclusive Leadership Insight 36: Inclusive leadership can be cultivated by being and knowing, and not just doing.

Support

Perceive your role as support rather than control and offer employees autonomy, independence, and adequate resources for their work (Carmeli et al., 2010; Hollander, 2009).

To promote an inclusive leadership style, it is important to view your role as a support rather than one of control or domination over your employees. Instead, your role needs to be centred around providing your employees with the autonomy, independence, and necessary resources to accomplish their work objectives, as Carmeli et al. (2010) and Hollander (2009) suggested.

Leaders who adopt this approach recognise the importance of supporting their employees in achieving success and focus on building strong relationships with their team members. Inclusive leadership fosters a positive, collaborative work environment, empowering employees to take ownership and providing necessary resources for success, unlike controlling leadership. By adopting a relational form of leadership, inclusive leaders prioritise their relationships with employees.

In doing so, they are empowered to be effective and successful in their roles. This approach ultimately benefits both the employees and the organisation as a whole, fostering a culture of collaboration and performance.

Inclusive Leadership Insight 37: Inclusive leadership is about supporting others to thrive.

Reality

Start with the reality of now, me, and us, rather than the phantasy of what should be as Kleinian theory alludes to. I apply this concept to inclusive leadership.

Inclusive leadership requires a pragmatic approach that begins with an honest appraisal of the current reality, as opposed to the idealised notion of what inclusion should look like. Around the childlike phantasies we all have as humans being natural, so too is the desire to aspire to a perfect, fully inclusive organisation. The practical reality is that this is a process of continuous improvement that requires attention to what is working, what is not, and how we can make progress towards greater inclusion.

Inclusive leaders understand that the pursuit of inclusion is a practice that involves using inclusion as a tool to create more effective work environments. By taking a pragmatic approach that focuses on achievable ideas and next steps, inclusive leaders are more adept at empowering their team members to work with the realities of the present moment. This approach helps to avoid the pitfalls of black-and-white thinking. With black-and-white thinking, there is a tendency to polarise situations into either good or bad. A realistic and pragmatic approach instead encourages a more nuanced and thoughtful perspective.

When leaders prioritise achievable ideas and actionable steps, they increase the opportunities for positive change and improved outcomes, such as higher employee engagement, retention, attraction, psychological safety, and performance, as well as fostering innovation and creativity. Ultimately, by grounding our actions in the reality of the present, we are better positioned to achieve our goals and make meaningful progress towards greater inclusion in the workplace.

Inclusive Leadership Insight 38: Inclusive leadership is about working with the reality of now and navigating the challenges rather than waiting for when the timing is right.

You

Randel et al. (2018) recommend actively developing leadership capacity for cognitive complexity, pro-diversity beliefs, and humility and further recommends that leaders actively develop their cognitive complexity, pro-diversity beliefs, and humility in order to embody inclusive leadership effectively. To achieve this, leaders need to focus on the three aspects of being, knowing, and doing, as previously discussed.

By adopting this approach, leaders can ensure that

their inclusive leadership is not merely a superficial, politically correct gesture but a genuine effort to address the complexities of diversity and inclusion within organisations. By actively cultivating their capacity for cognitive complexity, pro-diversity beliefs and humility, leaders can create a work environment that is truly inclusive and supportive of all employees while also fostering a culture of innovation and creativity.

Inclusive Leadership Insight 39: Inclusive leadership starts with you but is about other people.

CHAPTER 8: HOW CAN WE HAVE INCLUSIVE CONVERSATIONS AT WORK?

I facilitated sessions on inclusive conversations during a masterclass with the *British Psychological Society* in 2023. It was deemed as a highly sought-after topic. We discussed what *is* and *isn't* involved in inclusive conversations.

Most people who are interested in inclusive conversations are really looking for techniques or tactics in order for their conversation to be more inclusive. As conversations are relational and involve sharing information and messages, the approach to inclusive conversations varies based on the participants, topic, and communication styles. A more practical approach involves discussing common barriers and facilitators of inclusive dialogue, recognising that inclusive conversations are co-created and responsive, tailored to the specific individuals and content involved, rather than adhering to a universal set of considerations.

Common barriers to inclusive dialogue include:

☐ The conversation topic can have an impact on how a person experiences inclusion. What might be a barrier to inclusion, for instance, is if the content brings up shame or discomfort or has a lot of *shoulds* attached to it, then it will be harder to engage in an inclusive conversation because those experiences will influence how people are speaking, listening, and interpreting each other.

☐ Assumptions – All conversations have surrounding assumptions, both within them and around them. It's important to know that these assumptions of the people you are talking with, the content you're discussing, and the context in which you're having these discussions will influence whether this conversation is inclusive or not.

☐ Defensiveness – When we speak about defences, we're not just speaking about one psychological individual defence but also about group defences and defences of ego, reputation, and image. Within inclusive leadership and inclusive conversations, there are a lot of different dynamics at play, so a number of different offences can be barriers to an inclusive conversation.

☐ Jumping to conclusions – One of the fundamental distortions that affects most of our thinking is jumping to conclusions. We often jump to conclusions, focusing on patterns or assumptions rather than fully engaging with the topic at hand. This prevents us from actively listening to understand others' perspectives, inhibiting our ability to foster curiosity and engage in inclusive conversations. Inappropriate questions or statements, and one that comes up quite a bit on inclusion, is this discussion about what an appropriate or inappropriate statement question is. This will differ from the context of the relationship and the content of the discussion. However, it is inapt when an inappropriate question has been asked, as it can cause a great deal of discomfort for people involved as it can demonstrate a positionality or belief that an individual has and, therefore can shut down the openness.

☐ Fear of getting it wrong again – Linked to priorities and social class, this fear is tied to past experiences of criticism when making mistakes. Fear of being wrong can hinder asking the right questions. Addressing this involves preparation, taking responsibility, and prioritising learning over avoiding mistakes.

☐ Bad faith statements/questions – These encompass considerations such as individual perspectives, incompatible comparisons, or statements that misuse or manipulate inclusion efforts, diverting from their true purpose.

☐ Bias – Obviously, bias is a big one. I'm not going to say unconscious bias because, yes, that can be a barrier, but conscious bias can be too. So, all biases can be a barrier.

☐ Fixed mindsets occur when someone believes there's only one way to do things and that learning or growth isn't possible. This mindset can significantly restrict inclusive conversations as

157

individuals become entrenched in their own perspectives.

☐ Power struggles are another limitation or barrier to inclusive leadership because power struggles will prevent us from sharing power and continue to create a power-over-power approach.

☐ Denial of any wrongdoing or harm is a defence, but it comes up so much in inclusion work that it's important to mention it separately. If we deny or dismiss any wrongdoing conveyed to us, rather than processing it and considering how to address it, we automatically shut down inclusive conversations.

Common Factors for Inclusive Conversations

Conversely, there are factors that facilitate inclusive conversations. These involve taking personal responsibility, fostering self-awareness, adopting a growth mindset, sharing power, setting conversation boundaries, seeking consent, and considering the process, not just the content, such as evaluating the effectiveness of our discussion approach.

Listening to other people's points of view, especially when we disagree with them, being curious about what people are actually trying to communicate rather than getting hung up on the words they use or our interpretation of them and also engaging with more humility (Randel et al., 2018) and cognitive complexity, (Randel et al., 2018) are things can help inclusive conversations.

There are components that can help with inclusive conversations and are things you can practice or engage with in order to support a conversation to be more inclusive. Some of these components include the following –

- ✓ Understanding the boundaries and context.
- ✓ Using curiosity.
- ✓ Listening and sharing your perspective.
- ✓ Considering what is needed for people to feel included.
- ✓ Sharing power and avoiding universal right or wrong positions.
- ✓ Co-creating meaning and understanding.
- ✓ Creating belonging with a shared purpose to the conversation.
- ✓ Regulating oneself and reflection.

Inclusive Language

Encouraging inclusive language is crucial, but there's no universal standard for inclusive language. Inclusion evolves over time, so inclusive language requires ongoing consideration of principles rather than rigid rules.

Some of the things you need to consider for inclusive language include the following –

- No one group agrees on what language is inclusive for them, and no group is homogeneous.
- Language changes over time. This is important, as what was once inclusive may not be any longer.

- If you are aware of the harmful origins of a statement or phrase, it is helpful to find alternatives. If you are not, it is helpful to apologise and listen when told.
- Culturally speaking, different geographies find different languages harmful and inclusive.
- Inclusion is co-created. No one person can know everything about what includes another. It is interpersonal, so we need to co-create and learn about inclusive language together.
- Legislation has an impact on how people describe their identity.

However, there are some general shifts you can make to help your language be more inclusive. While I do not suggest that these are the only things you could do, I am also not suggesting that you should do them. Below are examples of what might be more helpful when trying to engage in more inclusive language –

- ✓ Rather than *boyfriend or girlfriend,* you could try *partner* if you aren't aware of an individual's partner's gender.
- ✓ Rather than *addict,* try someone *struggling with addiction* or someone who *misused substances.*
- ✓ Rather than *crazy,* you could try *wild.*
- ✓ Rather than *Mom or Dad,* you could try *parent or caregiver.*
- ✓ Rather than *homeless person,* you could try *person experiencing homelessness.*

There are also some very specific things that you can do to help improve your use of language, such as the following –

- Ask the person how they would like to be referred to or identified (when appropriate).
- Name the system of oppression rather than the person when unsure. E.g. people marginalised by race, sexuality, or people disabled by society. Keep the system of oppression front and centre.
- Ask the question, "I am not sure of the correct way to describe race/disability/gender/age, etc., in this situation. Can you help me?"

I work with people from different aspects of society. Whenever I work with people with different lived experiences of being marginalised, I've noticed that there are patterns and trends in their descriptions of how they experience inclusion or, more commonly, a lack of inclusion. I've compiled a broad list of challenges that people with lived experience of marginalisation and exclusion have shared with me over the past decade.

These include – When the other person needs to focus on the difference rather than staying connected to the purpose of the conversation. An example of this is if somebody came out or shared something about their identity that was traditionally marginalised, the individual would find ways to speak about that aspect of their identity rather than continuing the conversation related to the topic at hand. A notable example of this is when someone mentions being in a same-sex partnership, but instead of staying on topic, others divert the conversation by discussing their own same-sex friends or asking intrusive questions about their sexuality. These are unfounded expectations of needing to explain, justify, or behave like others with a shared identity. This stereotyping or assumption suggests that because we share a certain aspect of identity, we need to, therefore, share all aspects of it.

- ☐ "Thinking that just because we share an identity means we are the same or have the same opinions."
- ☐ "Asking me inappropriate questions that they wouldn't ask someone of a different identity."
- ☐ Deferring all questions related to a shared identity group to anyone in that identity group, even if we haven't chosen to engage.
- ☐ "Expecting me to speak on behalf of an entire group."
- ☐ Stereotyping a person by your understanding of their identity group.
- ☐ Referencing to an aspect of one's identity group when not relevant to the conversation.
- ☐ "Policing the language I use for myself or about my identity."

PART 4:
BUILDING INCLUSIVE
ORGANISATIONS

> *Tús maith, leath na hoibre – Your initial steps will dictate how well a project is going to go.*
>
> — An Irish Saying

For inclusive leadership to become normalised and ingrained in practice, we need to carefully consider how we socialise inclusion, inclusive leadership, and inclusive practices and processes. Often, ineffective ways to socialise inclusion result in inclusion not being integrated, but it can also result in people rejecting inclusion altogether.

One of the ways to avoid this is not to consider inclusion just as a topic but also how you are attempting to socialise and integrate inclusion. Inclusion within organisations differs from inclusion within society because there are different purposes and boundaries involved.

For instance, in society, you are a member of society whether you choose to be or not. There are multiple different facets, complexities, and intersections that exist within society. However, within an organisation, you don't just belong to the organisation. You belong to the organisation because you contribute to the organisation's purpose. This influences how we interpret and engage with inclusion at work. Understanding that inclusion in the workplace is about promoting and supporting the ultimate shared purpose allows you to socialise inclusion through the lens of support rather than a moral, political, or societal position.

With that in mind, I do not negate the fact that moral, political, and societal lenses influence inclusion within the workplace. However, I'm stating that working with inclusion from those perspectives within the limitations of an organisation often contributes to overwhelm and resistance. Within society, we don't have one agreed political, moral, or societal position, so to expect that we would create that within a workplace is unrealistic. Inclusion in the workplace needs to be directly related to achieving organisational goals and doing so through inclusive practises.

The following pages will be an introduction to different ways in which you can socialise and normalise inclusive practices as cultural norms in your organisation. With benefits that include –

- ✓ Improving team and organisational performance.
- ✓ Improving turnover and organisational sustainability.
- ✓ Attracting, retaining, and engaging key talent.
- ✓ Higher quality processes and outcomes.
- ✓ Effective leadership.
- ✓ Effective and enjoyable organisational culture.
- ✓ More individual commitment.

> "Some people only ask others to do something. I believe that, why should I wait for someone else? Why don't I take a step and move forward?"
>
> — Malala Yousafzai

CHAPTER 9: HOW CAN WE SOCIALISE INCLUSION AND INCLUSIVE LEADERSHIP IN ORGANISATIONS?

Organisations, even prior to founding, have to choose their structure, and this structure directly impacts what good looks like.

Not-for-profits aim to support a group of people and have an obligation to those they serve. This is often aligned with equality (Whitman, 2009).

The public/state aims to support the running of the country from a particular perspective and has an obligation to citizens. Public organisations (Moore et al., 2021) have a political mandate to meet their citizen's needs.

For-profit aims to provide profit and has an obligation to create profits for stakeholders and owners.

Things that impact socialising inclusion in an organisation include organisational purpose/task, legislation, power distribution, culture, geographical location, societal *norms*, workplace *norms*, and workforce access. Hence, the reason for the book's subtitle, *Navigating Organisational Complexity,* is that when we bring inclusion to life in organisations, we need to accept and work with the reality that there are complexities within organisational inclusion. Therefore, the only way to practice inclusive leadership or co-create inclusive organisations is to navigate these complexities rather than become frustrated or reductionist in our approach.

What Helps Organisations Be Inclusive?

Some of the ways that can help organisations be inclusive include –

- Perceive inclusion as behavioural norms and practices and not political beliefs, values, or feelings.
- Work appropriately with beliefs, values, and feelings.
- Leave room for differences and unite people on the task and purpose.
- Develop people's capacity to co-create inclusive experiences (uniqueness, belonging, psychological safety).
- Use the organisation's vision, mission, and values to guide decisions.
- Start with where you are and not the *phantasy* of what it should be.
- Use strength-focused approaches.
- Make inclusion an integrated aspect of *how* we do business and achieve results.

- Tie inclusion to good results. See it as a process, not a goal (like health and safety, introduction of tech, exercise).

A prevalent issue in fostering inclusion within organisations arises when initiatives take an activist approach, aiming to challenge established systems. Despite good intentions, this may conflict with environments focused on profit-making, healthcare provision, or education, appearing counterproductive to the organisation's core objectives. Instead, the focus could be on aligning inclusion efforts with the organisation's mission, values, and current objectives. In doing so, these efforts could be made more palatable and integrated into the fabric of organisational operations without inciting division or resistance.

For this purpose, it's vital to pivot away from initiatives that, despite their positive intentions, yield minimal real-world change and instead adopt evidence-based practices. For example, while unconscious bias training is popular, its effectiveness remains debated, and it does not necessarily address the root issues of bias in the workplace. Changing individual beliefs, especially without consent, can be both oppressive and counterproductive.

In change processes, there are often three camps: the *yes*, the *no*, and *the I don't know*. Those who agree will embrace it, those who disagree may resist openly or subtly, and those who are unsure will observe and choose their stance based on self-interest. I am specifically speaking about the assumption that unconscious bias training is going to change behaviours at work.

In many workplaces, while there's an increase in political correctness, biases persist. If unconscious bias training were effective, we would see improvements in various aspects like demographic representation, interviews, promotions, meetings, and relationships across the organisation. I know that too much chocolate is not the most nutritious food and will have consequences, but chocolate is an easy yes for me, and I will continue to eat it. Knowledge doesn't result in behaviour change. It is part of a change process but, for some reason, has been positioned in unconscious bias training as the way to get less bias in our workplaces.

Change also has many aspects to it, but fundamentally, I think it has two core avenues for people in workplaces: a desire that is bigger than the effort required or a desire to avoid undesirable consequences. These two different motivations for change mean that unconscious bias training is unlikely to be enough for any substantial change efforts.

Nevertheless, a more effective approach involves working with desire and consequences in our change efforts, establishing clear standards for behaviour, communication, and task completion that support the organisation's goals while incorporating inclusive practices into achieving those goals.

This strategy avoids the pitfalls of attempting to homogenise beliefs and instead focuses on actionable, observable standards that facilitate an inclusive work environment. It recognises that while personal beliefs may vary, workplace behaviour needs to adhere to principles that foster inclusion and equality, as dictated by local legislation and organisational policy.

Another aspect we need to consider is what should be prioritised in the inclusion journey. It's crucial not to merely focus on what is popular or appealing to us but rather to identify what is necessary. The question then becomes, "What is the most significant barrier to inclusion within your organisation currently and how addressing this could lead to the greatest impact?" This perspective encourages us to view inclusion through a lens of impact rather than solely identity.

For instance, including a specific group may seem like a straightforward approach. However, a more impactful strategy might involve enhancing understanding and support for diverse contributions and communication styles. By improving expectations around communication and how individuals with different experiences contribute and add value, we can move beyond normalising a singular approach. This could lead to a more inclusive experience for various marginalised groups without resorting to stereotypes or targeted inclusion, which sometimes provokes discussions around tokenism.

The suggestion here is not to diminish the specific needs of different groups but to examine our workforce, identify who is missing, consider how their inclusion could bring value, and assist those within the organisation who have unmet inclusion needs. Inclusion operates through consistent mechanisms, regardless of group-specific needs. By employing these mechanisms effectively, we develop the capacity for inclusivity in our communication, behaviour, and task completion, leading towards a genuinely inclusive organisation.

However, focusing solely on identity-based inclusion can lead to challenges and competition among different identity groups, a situation already visible in many contexts. Mimicking the strategies of other countries or organisations without considering the unique aspects of our context – such as changing times, differing legislations, and distinct historical backgrounds – can be problematic. Inclusion is a complex issue that is not resolved through simple technical solutions but requires cognitive complexity and a nuanced approach.

Viewing inclusion as a dynamic and ongoing process that permeates every aspect of our work is essential. It supports us in conducting our tasks more robustly and effectively, moving beyond mere box-ticking or demographic counting. Continuous learning and adaptation are key, enabling us to navigate the complexities of organisational life and truly embrace inclusion.

When organisations claim inclusivity, it prompts reflection on what inclusivity means to them. Does it imply a series of completed checklists, a host of social activities or a genuine effort to embrace and respond to differences in a way that adds value to the organisation's purpose? It raises questions about whose perspectives are considered and whether there is a shared understanding of inclusivity across all levels of the organisation, from those who are marginalised to those in leadership positions. This is a crucial consideration for anyone working towards creating more inclusive environments.

Inclusion needs to be viewed as a dynamic, ongoing process that is integral to all aspects of organisational functioning. It requires a commitment to continuous learning and adaptation, moving beyond mere tokenistic measures to genuinely embrace the complexities and nuances of creating an inclusive environment. This perspective challenges organisations to reflect critically on what it means to be inclusive, ensuring that it is not just a superficial label but a deeply embedded practice that enhances the organisation's purpose and value through its embrace of diversity.

Ultimately, the goal is to cultivate an organisational culture where inclusion is woven into the very fabric of daily operations, informed by a nuanced understanding of its multifaceted nature and the various factors that influence its implementation. By doing so, organisations can move beyond simplistic or tick-box solutions to embrace the true complexity of inclusion, thereby enriching the workplace for all its members.

Bringing Inclusion to Life

Several factors influence organisational inclusion, and these are always present in organisations. Organisational purpose directly impacts how we think about inclusion. The professions within the organisation influence the values engaged, as well as the legislation that governs the organisation, the industry it sits within, how the organisation structures power, and the workforce the organisation has access to, as well as its culture and workplace norms. Other factors include the geographical reach of the organisation's customers and employees and the social norms and expectations at play for those employees and customers.

Bringing inclusion to life within the workplace involves a comprehensive approach that transcends mere policy implementation. It touches on the essence of organisational culture and practice. According to Wilson (2023), addressing the eight inclusion *Needs of All People*, I have expanded insights into how to actualise these principles based on work I have done with organisations, utilising Wilson's paper.

Integrating an Inclusive Lens in All Policies and Procedures:

Beyond the specific policies dedicated to inclusion, it's imperative to embed an inclusive perspective across all organisational policies and procedures. This means reviewing and adapting processes, from recruitment and onboarding to performance evaluations and promotions, ensuring they are fair, equitable, and accessible to everyone. Such integration demonstrates a commitment to inclusion at the systemic level, impacting every aspect of the organisation's operations.

Integrating Inclusive Practices in All Settings and at Every Opportunity:

Inclusion should permeate all areas of the organisation, including informal settings and interactions. This involves creating spaces where diverse voices are heard and valued, ensuring that inclusivity is not confined to structured meetings or training sessions but is evident in daily practices, social interactions, and decision-making processes.

Middle and Senior Management Rewarded for Being Inclusive and Developing Inclusive Skills:

To foster a culture of inclusion, it's crucial that middle and senior management are not only encouraged to practice inclusivity but are also recognised and rewarded for this purpose. This could include incentives for completing inclusive leadership training, successfully leading diverse teams, or implementing innovative, inclusive practices. Such recognition helps to embed inclusion as a core leadership competency.

Formal Senior Leaders Championing Inclusion Efforts and Role Modelling Best Practice:

Senior leaders play a pivotal role in setting the tone for organisational culture. When they actively champion inclusion efforts and model inclusive behaviours, they send a powerful message about the organisation's values. This leadership commitment can inspire others within the organisation to follow suit, creating a ripple effect that promotes inclusivity at all levels.

Fostering a Learning Environment, So Mistakes Are Seen as Part of the Process and Not a Looming Threat:

Cultivating an environment where learning from mistakes is encouraged is essential for innovation and growth. This approach supports inclusion by allowing individuals to explore, experiment, and contribute without fear of retribution for errors. Such an environment fosters psychological safety where team members feel secure in expressing themselves and taking risks.

Using Coaching Approaches in Conversations:

Implementing coaching techniques in conversations across the organisation promotes a culture of empathy, active listening, and personal development. This approach facilitates more meaningful interactions, encourages self-reflection, and supports individual growth, contributing to a more inclusive organisational climate.

Raising Awareness of Inclusion, Psychological Safety, and its Relationship with Team and Organisational Performance:

Educating all members of the organisation about the importance of inclusion and psychological safety and their impact on performance is vital. Understanding these concepts helps individuals see the value of diverse perspectives and fosters a sense of belonging, which in turn can enhance team cohesion and overall organisational effectiveness.

By embedding these principles into the fabric of the organisation, businesses can create a more inclusive culture that not only meets the needs of their diverse workforce but also enhances organisational performance through the richness of diverse thought, increased engagement, and innovation.

Inclusive Strategies

People are always asking for advice and technical solutions when inclusion really requires strategic approaches. These approaches allow us to embed important changes and not simply rush to something at the moment when it is only waiting to appear again. Here are some strategies that, when strategically positioned, can start to shaft us from reductionist solutions and start us engaging with the emergent and complex reality of inclusive leadership. These aren't quick wins. They are about seeing how to build inclusive leadership into how you do things and taking a more strategic view than reactive.

Here are a number of strategies that support inclusion coming to life within an organisation –

>> Making time to discuss issues when they arise.
>> Supporting and encouraging employees with queries and concerns. Don't just brush them off.
>> Practising active listening, open questions, and listening to all voices during meetings.
>> Building trust within individuals and teams.
>> Consistent and clear communication.
>> Focusing on the strengths and differences team members bring and how they can add value.

» Accepting fault when appropriate and aiming to do better.
» Following up with less active staff to ask for their contribution and preferred ways of engaging in meetings.
» Consciously connecting with people who are not the same as you.
» Encouraging and seeking reverse mentoring opportunities.
» Catching your own assumptions about others and self-educating on microaggressions and unconscious bias.
» Working towards creating a psychologically safe learning environment and providing a safe space for employees to feel valued.
» Hiring from a wide variety of backgrounds.
» Praising efforts more than criticising.
» Considerate scheduling (considering personal lives, work hours, religious, care and community needs)
» Frequently assessing the pay structure and compensation benefits.
» Supporting cross-departmental relationships.
» Creating a system for addressing misunderstandings and resolving disagreements.

Focus on the Benefits

Linking inclusion to the tangible benefits it can bring to the workplace is a highly effective approach to promoting its adoption. It is important to recognise that inclusive leadership should not be viewed as an isolated endpoint but rather as a means of achieving improved outcomes that align with the goals and objectives of the organisation. When inclusive practices are framed in this way, individuals within the organisation are more likely to recognise the inherent value of engaging with them. This approach positions inclusion as a *value-adding* component that supports the larger mission rather than an additional task or burden. As a result, individuals are reassured by the understanding that inclusive practices can improve outcomes, contribute positively to the overall task at hand, and connect more closely to what is in it for them.

Inclusion as a practice and process, not a result, leads to more –

- Psychological safety
- Innovation
- Creativity
- Employee engagement
- Student engagement
- Fairer and equitable outcomes and processes
- Effective work cultures
- More robust results
- Improved excellence

Start with Me

> *"The energies of wisdom, compassion, inclusiveness, fearlessness, patience, and non-discrimination – never disparaging anyone – are all the qualities of awakened beings. Cultivating."*
>
> — Thich Nhat Hanh

When striving to promote socialisation and normalise inclusivity, it is essential to first examine our own relationship with inclusivity. This requires us to reflect on the ways in which our thoughts, behaviours, and actions are aligned with an inclusive approach.

Below is a list of reflective questions that may help you identify development opportunities –

» In what ways do I prioritise diversity and inclusivity in my personal and professional life?

» How do my beliefs and values align with promoting inclusivity, and what tangible steps have I taken to implement them?

» Am I aware of my unconscious biases, and how do I actively work to mitigate their impact on my decision-making?

» How do I engage with people who are different from me, and how do I ensure that they feel welcome and included?

» What steps have I taken to learn about different cultures, identities and experiences, and how do I incorporate this knowledge into my interactions and decision-making?

» How do I acknowledge and celebrate the diverse perspectives and talents of those around me?

» How do I react when someone raises concerns about inclusivity, and how do I ensure that their concerns are heard and addressed?

» Have I ever made assumptions about someone based on their identity, and how did I rectify the situation?

» How do I use my privilege to advocate for and amplify the voices of those who experience marginalisation?

» What steps can I take to continue to grow my inclusivity and promote a more inclusive environment in my personal and professional life?

Raising Group Awareness and Supporting the Task

Frequently, when we attempt to raise awareness of inclusion in group settings, we tend to focus on discrimination instead of inclusion. While this may be appropriate in certain circumstances, this approach can trigger defensiveness when the topic of inclusion arises. When approached reactively, the language of inclusion may inadvertently be conflated with discrimination as it implies the need for corrective action.

A more effective approach would be to normalise the use of non-blaming questions and statements that stimulate curiosity about whether inclusivity is being considered. Using a more inclusive approach, we can shift the focus from solely addressing discrimination to promoting a culture of inclusion.

For example, individuals could use the following examples (or come up with their own) that align with their personal, cultural, and preference norms –

» "I wonder if there is a way we could make this more inclusive?"

» "Have we considered how this might impact those who are frequently overlooked?"

» "Can you help me understand how this policy is inclusive?"
» "I am not sure about this. Could we be unintentionally excluding anyone?"
» "I feel as though we are not considering XYZ."
» "Could we do this in a more inclusive way?"
» "Are we ignoring anyone?"
» "Are we neglecting anyone's needs?"
» "Is this the most robust option?"
» "Are we too homogenous in our conclusion?"
» "Is groupthink present?"

Organisational Performance

Ní neart go cur le chéile – There is no strength without unity.

— An Irish Saying

The relationship between inclusion, inclusive leadership and organisational performance is profound and multifaceted, with substantial evidence suggesting that fostering an inclusive environment contributes significantly to a range of positive outcomes for organisations. The points highlighted below offer a deeper insight into how inclusion and inclusive leadership catalyse organisational success.

An Increase in Innovation and Creativity: Research by Javed et al. (2018, 2020) and others (Zhu et al., 2020; Qi et al., 2019; Falih Bannay et al., 2020) demonstrates that inclusive environments, where diverse perspectives are valued and integrated, lead to heightened levels of innovation and creativity. This diversity of thought enables organisations to solve complex problems more effectively and to think outside traditional parameters, fostering a culture of continuous improvement and adaptation.

Psychologically Healthy Organisations Experience Significantly Lower Staff Turnover: According to the *American Psychological Association* (APA, 2014), organisations that prioritise psychological health report five times less staff turnover. This underscores the importance of supportive workplaces where employees feel valued, understood, and secure, contributing to higher levels of employee retention and reducing the costs associated with turnover.

Inclusive Leadership and Organisational Citizenship Behaviour: The study by Tran, T. B. H., & Choi, S. B. (2019) highlights the positive correlation between inclusive leadership and organisational citizenship behaviour. Inclusive leaders who promote fairness, diversity, and open communication cultivate an environment where employees are more likely to go above and beyond their job requirements, contributing to the overall success and cohesion of the organisation.

Enhanced Market Capture and Competitive Advantage: Organisations that embrace diversity and inclusion are 70 per cent more likely to capture new markets (2018 CEPC Whitepaper, *Diversity & Inclusion in Corporate Social Engagement*). This increased market share is likely due to the organisation's ability to understand and cater to a broader range of customer needs and preferences, driven by the diverse insights of its workforce.

Superior Team Effectiveness, Innovation, and Customer Service: According to the Inclusion @ Work Index 21/22 from Australia, teams in inclusive environments are significantly more likely to be effective, innovative, and provide excellent customer service. These teams are also more satisfied, more committed to their work and less likely to leave their jobs, indicating a strong link between inclusion and job satisfaction, loyalty, and performance excellence.

Reduced Negative Impact on Mental Health and Discrimination: Inclusive workplaces are associated with a reduced negative impact on employees' mental health and lower instances of discrimination and harassment. This creates a safer and more supportive environment for all employees, contributing to their overall well-being and performance.

Increased Collaboration between Team Members: Bourke & Titus (2019) found that teams in inclusive settings are 29 per cent more likely to report high levels of collaboration. This enhanced collaboration stems from a culture of trust and openness, where diverse ideas are encouraged and valued, leading to more effective teamwork and problem-solving.

These findings collectively underscore the tangible benefits of inclusion and inclusive leadership on organisational performance. By fostering an environment where diversity is embraced and all individuals feel included, organisations can unlock their full potential, achieving higher levels of innovation, employee satisfaction, and market competitiveness.

Do Not Privilege Confidence in Your Workplace; Focus on Competence.

Confidence and competence are often confused and wrongly associated with one another. Tomas Chamorro states a great distinction between confidence and competence, "Competence is how good you are at something. Confidence is how good you THINK you are at something."

Often, confidence is influenced by societal experiences of being the *right kind of person* or *what we expect*. Confidence is also someone's self-belief in how they can complete a task, and it has very little to do with their ability. We see demographic differences concerning confidence that are not linked to competence. This is strongly correlated with gender research. Studies show that men often appear much more confident. However, this does not always correlate to their competence. Women, on the other hand, were often shown to downplay their competence and also have less confidence in job interviews. All genders could present one way and be another, but the above statement is based on a statical difference in two identity groups, not a generalisation.

Telling people to be more confident ignores the fact that confidence can be a tightrope for some identities. Too much or too little should not be used as a rationale for decisions. It ignores that a person's identity has a direct impact on social expectations and, therefore, how they are viewed and what is deemed appropriate for them. Obviously, this is mostly invisible and unconscious, so it can take a bit to embrace. From an inclusive leadership perspective, not only does the leadership you offer need to be inclusive, but also your understanding of how your identity and positionality may influence what results in effective and ineffective leadership.

We like confident people because it makes us feel safe and because we have been taught to trust confidence and charisma. However, we also know confidence is closely aligned with the dark triad in leadership when we view it through the charisma lens.

When we assume confidence means trust and competency and that we are in a safe pair of hands, we indirectly give an advantage to anyone who has been reaffirmed in society and a disadvantage to others who have had more critique from society. Yet, it has little or nothing to do with their competence. Highly competent people may or may not be confident about their skills, while non-competent people may or may not be confident.

Additionally, it is also a right for some identities that are confident to be rewarded. In contrast, for other identities, it is considered *getting above their station*, *cocky, too big for their boots* and so on.

While there is so much evidence of it for gender, there are equally some concerning examples about racial and ethnic differences, which play a big part in the tightrope also. For some racial and ethnic identities, confidence is considered *automatic* and even expected (usually for white people. However. it is important to know that this may differ based on context), while for other racial and ethnic identities, it is considered *aggressive*, *pushy* or *loud*.

Normalising Inclusion Conversations

There are several ways we can normalise inclusive conversations. The following are examples that may help you bring inclusion into your discussions more effectively outside of blame, shame or a reaction.

We can proactively normalise inclusive conversations by initiating them.

Here are some examples –
Share as we learn by

- ✓ Demonstrating that we don't need to be all-knowing.
- ✓ Demonstrating that we are on a journey.
- ✓ Demonstrating that it's okay to be learning and to get it wrong.

Sharing when we learn that something is harmful with statements such as "I didn't realise this was hurtful/harmful," "I didn't know this was racist/sexist," or "I only just learned that XYZ" can help normalise the conversation.

Consider barriers

In decision-making and conversation, normalise asking questions about the social or structural barriers that may be in place, even when it isn't directly an issue for you.
Examples include: "Is that building accessible?" or "Does this learning design consider Universal Design for Learning Principles?"

Psychological Safety

The concept of psychological safety, where team members feel safe to take risks and be vulnerable in front of each other, is crucial for fostering a culture of inclusion and innovation within the workplace. Research indicates that inclusive leadership plays a significant role in enhancing work engagement and establishing psychological safety among employees. Below is an expanded exploration of the key points that illustrate how organisations can cultivate psychological safety through inclusive leadership practices.

Inclusive Leadership as a Strong Predictor for Work Engagement and Psychological Safety *(Aslan et al., 2021):* This highlights the critical role of leaders in creating environments where employees feel engaged and psychologically safe. Leaders need to actively foster inclusivity by respecting and valuing diverse perspectives, encouraging open communication, and demonstrating empathy towards team members.

Positive Association Between Leader Inclusiveness and Members' Perceptions of Psychological Safety *(Hirak et al., 2012):* Leaders who embrace inclusiveness directly impact their team members' feelings of safety and belonging. This involves creating a team atmosphere where individuals are comfortable expressing their thoughts without fear of negative repercussions.

The Mediating Role of Caring Ethical Climate and Psychological Safety *(Xintian Li, Peng Peng, 2022):* A caring ethical climate, nurtured by inclusive leadership, can reduce emotional exhaustion and enhance psychological safety. Leaders should strive to establish ethical standards that prioritise empathy, respect, and consideration for the well-being of all employees.

Developing Humility, Pro-diversity Beliefs and Cognitive Complexity: Leaders should commit to ongoing personal development in areas such as humility, appreciation of diversity, and the ability to understand complex, multifaceted issues. This approach encourages a leadership style that values learning from others and acknowledges the benefits of diverse perspectives.

Leading by Sharing Common Goals and Aspirations: Focusing on shared objectives helps to unite teams, transcending individual differences. Leaders should communicate these goals clearly and demonstrate how each team member's contributions are vital to achieving them.

Inviting People to Formal and Informal Interactions: Encouraging both structured and casual interactions among team members can foster a sense of community and belonging, which are critical components of psychological safety.

Considering Inclusion from a Needs and Performance Perspective: Inclusion efforts should be tailored to meet individual needs and align with organisational performance goals. This balanced approach ensures that inclusivity directly contributes to the organisation's success.

Supporting Different Points of View Without Privileging One Over the Other: Leaders need to create an environment where diverse opinions are welcomed and valued equally, promoting a culture of mutual respect and understanding.

Using Organisational Purpose, Values, and Vision to Inform Decisions: Decisions should be grounded in the organisation's foundational principles, ensuring alignment with its broader mission and promoting a cohesive, inclusive culture.

Focusing on Behaviour, Communication and Task at Hand: Prioritising actions and interactions that contribute to team goals rather than shared personal values or beliefs helps to maintain a focus on performance and inclusivity.

Understanding People Do Their Best Work Differently: Recognising and facilitating individual work styles enables team members to perform optimally, contributing to a more adaptable and resilient organisation.

Appreciating That Differences Add Value: A genuine appreciation for diversity can transform differences from potential sources of conflict into opportunities for innovation and growth.

Setting Others Up to Succeed in the Way They Need: Tailoring support to meet individual team members' needs demonstrates a commitment to their success and well-being.

Taking Feedback on and Addressing Behaviour: Constructive feedback is essential for personal and professional development. Leaders should be open to receiving feedback and willing to address any behaviours that may hinder inclusivity.

Raising Awareness of Your Own Norms and Assumptions: Leaders should continuously reflect on their own biases and assumptions, striving to overcome them to foster a more inclusive environment.

Inviting People to Contribute in Ways They Feel Comfortable: Encouraging team members to share their insights and ideas in ways they find most comfortable can enhance participation and engagement.

By integrating these practices, organisations can create a culture where psychological safety is prioritised, leading to enhanced engagement, innovation, and overall performance. Inclusive leadership is not just a strategy but a fundamental principle that underpins a thriving, resilient and cohesive workplace environment.

Employee Engagement

The impact of inclusive leadership and a psychologically healthy organisational culture on team and organisational performance is significant, as evidenced by research findings. Teams and organisations that prioritise psychological health and inclusivity see remarkable improvements in performance, decision-making quality, collaboration, employee engagement, and retention. Expanding on these points offers a comprehensive view of how inclusivity and psychological health are critical to organisational success.

Increased Likelihood of High Performance: According to Bourke & Titus (2019), teams in inclusive environments are 17 per cent more likely to report high performance. This suggests that when team members feel valued and included, they are more motivated and likely to contribute their best efforts, leading to enhanced overall performance.

Enhanced Decision-Making Quality: The same study found that teams are 20 per cent more likely to believe they make high-quality decisions. Inclusive environments that welcome diverse perspectives foster more comprehensive and well-considered decision-making processes, reducing the risk of oversight and enhancing the quality of outcomes.

Improved Collaboration: Teams in inclusive settings are 29 per cent more likely to report behaving collaboratively (Bourke & Titus, 2019). Inclusion promotes a sense of belonging and respect among team members, facilitating effective collaboration and teamwork. This collaborative behaviour is essential for leveraging diverse skills and insights, leading to innovative solutions and a competitive edge.

Lower Staff Turnover in Psychologically Healthy Organisations: Organisations that prioritise psychological health experience five times less staff turnover (APA, 2014). A supportive and healthy workplace reduces stress, burnout, and dissatisfaction among employees, significantly improving retention rates. This stability is crucial for maintaining organisational knowledge and reducing the costs associated with recruiting and training new staff.

Positive Relationship Between Inclusive Leadership and Work Engagement: Research by Choi, S., Tran, T., & Park, B. (2015) demonstrates that inclusive leadership is positively related to employee work engagement. Leaders who practice inclusivity foster an environment where employees feel empowered, valued, and connected to their work, leading to higher levels of engagement and performance.

Organisations thrive on the contributions of their employees, and creating a connection between employees and their workplace is essential for avoiding the pitfalls of a disengaged and unproductive workforce. Inclusive leadership is not just a moral imperative but a strategic necessity for attracting and retaining top talent and encouraging them to perform at their best. It acts as a powerful countermeasure against negative behaviours and practices in the workplace, such as discrimination, exclusion, and unethical behaviour.

Implementing inclusive leadership practices involves recognising and valuing the unique contributions of each employee, fostering open and respectful communication, and creating opportunities for all team members to grow and succeed. By doing so, organisations can create a supportive, engaging and psychologically safe environment that not only attracts but also retains high-calibre employees committed to achieving their best work. This approach leads to improved organisational outcomes, including higher performance levels, better decision-making, and more effective collaboration, all of which contribute to the long-term success and sustainability of the organisation.

CHAPTER 10: HOW CAN WE USE INCLUSION AND LEVERAGE POLICY FOR A MEANINGFUL IMPACT?

This chapter has been graciously contributed by Lynn Killick of Leading Kind.

> *"Politically astute, not politically correct."*
>
> — Leading Kind

That's the *Leading Kind* strapline and one that occasionally causes alarm. Why do I, co-founder of an organisation promoting inclusive workplaces, approach my work this way? Because I deliver results and drive change.

In this chapter, I begin by explaining why taking a pragmatic approach that considers the political environment (small p and big P) and is informed by evidence is key to creating a foundation to support an inclusive culture and policy environment that improves outcomes for people. I also set out some lessons for leaders based on my experience and what I have learned and continue to learn from others.

So, Why Pragmatism Over Idealism?

Being politically astute is often described as the art of getting things done in the midst of conflict. Working to advance equality requires a juggling of identities in the context of social change and business and varying levels of leadership, confidence, and competence. By itself, the opportunities for and presence of conflicts are significant. For example –

- The positioning of *equality groups* – a battle akin to an ongoing game of Top Trumps™.
- The battle between the EDI enthusiasts and the leaders and managers for whom it isn't a priority.
- The frustrations of top teams wishing to progress on issues of DEI but are seeing lots of activity with no impact and finding it difficult to harness energy in the right direction.
- The challenge of the *right on* board who want to do something about the current societal hot topic but are blind to evidence about the persistent inequalities in the workplace, which might not be as *sexy* or topical.

In my experience, a version of all these things can be going on at once within an organisational eco-system. To manage these competing demands and challenges, it is necessary to start from a position of reality.

Many people talk about diversity maturity, but getting work done on diversity isn't a linear path of growth.

Let's be frank, work on inclusion isn't new. Every organisation should be getting it right by now.

So, before we get started, here is some context and clarification of what I mean by inclusion – without any reference to different types of shoes or metaphors about different height boxes to help see *the game* over the fence.

Much of my experience and practice is informed by finding the systemic barriers that exclude people from reaching their potential and working out how to dismantle these and build better solutions for the benefit of everyone.

When I talk about inclusion, I am referring to two specific phenomena: *The first* relates to leaders creating the conditions that attract and retain the best people to help their organisations thrive. The default assumption is that decision-making is improved in teams that are made up of heterogeneous rather than homogeneous groups.

The second relates to the fact that demographic diversity on its own won't shift the dial (Edmans, 2023), and leaders need to understand how to create cultures where colleagues at every level have a voice. Detert and Burris (2007:1) define voice as "The discretionary provision of information intended to improve organisational functioning" and assumes reciprocal benefit for those who speak up and those who have the authority to act on what they hear. For those interested in the employee voice research, they will find the work of Macleod and Clark's (2009) review of employee engagement informative as it highlights that voice is the least well-researched driver of employee engagement. Studies by Purcell (2014) and Wilkinson (2014), through to a recent literature review by Mohammed et al. (2023), highlight the impact of employee voice on employees' morale, motivation, well-being and ultimately, the contribution to performance and organisational effectiveness.

Essentially, whether employees perceive they *have a say* in decisions that affect them and how they choose to express their voice is important for both individual well-being and organisational performance. From my perspective, it is the foundation of real inclusion.

The good news is that there are many ways to involve and include people for mutual benefit. The bad news is that there is no standard playbook or formula that can be applied. Your role as an inclusive leader is to expect the unexpected and to learn that applying solutions that are based on stereotypes can be counterproductive. Any approach should, as far as possible, be data – and insight-driven and informed by voices inside and outside the organisation.

This is not to say that there shouldn't be a coherent strategy to get from A to B. There should be. However, to achieve the objective – the best impact – the route might need to take several twists and turns before reaching the desired outcome. This is what I mean by pragmatism. It is more like knowing there is no set recipe and more a set of ingredients that can be adapted according to taste. I am drifting into metaphors here, but hopefully, it gives you a flavour of what I mean.

And if you are going to get it right, this is what you need to do –

Look, Listen, Look Again

The first lesson is to build a baseline. Start by crossing the road to get the ingredients you need. Look, listen, look again.

Look

» Establish what you know and try to work out what you don't know.

» A first step is the generation of data. What size and shape are your workforce, and what are the characteristics of your applicants and employees? Who are your customers?

» The second step is giving this data context, transforming the numbers into information. Who isn't sharing personal data, what data gaps do we have, who is missing, who isn't progressing, who isn't buying?

» The critical step is turning the information you now hold into knowledge. Knowledge has long been described as the capacity to act (Dawson, 1999; Stehr, 2005). The inclusive leader can change the capacity to act into deliberate action. More on this later.

Listen

Data and statistics are only part of the picture when trying to understand inclusion in the workplace. I tend to agree with Andrew Lang's adaptation of Hausman's quote that when it comes to diversity data, "People use statistics as a drunken man uses lampposts, for support, rather than for illumination."

I believe the key to understanding and acting, transforming your information into knowledge, is by listening to people.

A recent *Harvard Review Business* article highlights the positive impact of independently facilitated focus groups to engage employees on issues of inclusion (Brown, 2023), and this chimes with my experience. I use focus groups and deep dive 1-2-1 interviews to ensure that employee voice is central to figuring out what organisation inclusion priorities should be (people tell us what the inequalities are and where they need more skills). Likewise, engaging with people uncovers the great practice, the things that are going well and need to be shared, adapted, and adopted to work across other areas of the business.

Once the conversation has started and people can see that their insights have been listened to and are being acted on, it opens the routes for improved channels for employee voice. Our data suggests this has a positive impact on employee engagement, which we know is linked to improved performance.

Look again

Certainly, there will be a requirement to assess alterations in data and to gauge the effects of implemented actions, but what I'm emphasising here is examination. Oversight. Responsibility. Our research has shown that effective scrutiny is key to achieving inclusion and is central to inclusive leadership regardless of what level.

>> At an individual level, how do you show your inclusion impact through the performance review or appraisal process? How is action on inclusion recognised?

>> At a team level, how have we embedded inclusion in our activities that contribute to the strategic goals of the organisation?

> » At a corporate level, have we progressed against the persistent inequalities or equality KPIs that we have set?
> » At a governance level, do we understand the experience behind the numbers? Is no news good news or a concern?

So, *Look Again* is about asking the right questions at the right level, what I call conscious scrutiny. I'll provide more detail about this towards the end of the chapter.

The Right Foundations for Inclusion with Impact

These three key moves of *Look – Listen – Look Again* sound simple, but in my experience, one of the key issues that hinder progress in advancing equality is the lack of skills or authority among those in EDI roles. I often find that individuals tasked with implementing work on diversity and inclusion do not possess the necessary combination of expertise or decision-making power to bring about meaningful transformation. A reliance on enthusiasm and passion without the ability to make impactful decisions or influence organisational culture means that these individuals are often limited in their ability to effect real change. It is crucial, therefore, that we empower those at the forefront of this work with the skills needed to drive the change needed.

The nuts and bolts of equality law can be learned. Of course, the *diversity and inclusion* chip is important. People need the fire in the belly, and the ethical understanding of why work on inclusion is important and necessary. However, I would argue that the skills required to do the job well relate to change management and knowledge transfer. An EDI professional should always be trying to do themselves out of the job, empowering others to gain knowledge and to *do*. The upside for EDI professionals is that action on inclusion is always needed. By taking a change management approach, there is increased scope for development and career progression.

You mainstream work on equality by sharing the load, not gatekeeping the knowledge.

The second lesson is to frame the foundation for change. So, as an inclusive leader, you need to understand what you need. What skills are required? Where should this person or team *sit* in your structure? Is HR the best home? Can a Head of EDI influence *up* if it's the people, policies, and processes that need to change to remove the barriers present at application and progression?

My recommendation is that there needs to be a route to the executive, which might be through reporting lines for an individual or a team or through a committee route, but the executive needs to know what's working well and what issues are on the horizon that it may need to grapple with.

The skills I would look for in individuals working in EDI are:

- ✓ **Political Acuity** – do they know what to flag, when to flag, and how to raise awareness of issues that are likely to affect your business? Do they understand connections, internal and external, to the organisation that might enhance or inhibit your work on inclusion?
- ✓ **Change Management** – Do they know how to effect change?

✓ **Influence** – Do they know how to bring people with divergent views together and create win-win scenarios?

✓ **Communication** – Do they understand the fundamentals of inclusive communication?

✓ **Policy Development** – Do they know how to access and apply evidence to inform policy and decision-making?

✓ **Impact** – If this isn't their first job, what is the biggest difference they have made? What was the impact on people? What inequality did they address, and what systemic change did they influence?

Assuming you've worked out the structure and the skills required to get the right people in the right place, the continuing challenge is sense-checking the expert. In the course of 2023 and already in the first months of 2024, it is clear that the term EDI expert might require just more than a pinch of salt. In light of the number of tribunals and awards made for decisions about *inclusion,* whether that was about allowing an individual to be mobbed for the beliefs they hold (Meade v Open University Tribunal, 2024) or dismissing someone for asking a question without malintent but using inappropriate language in doing so (Borg Neale v Lloyds Tribunal, 2023).

These cases add to the evidence that well-intentioned (I hope) work on inclusion has unfortunately led to exclusion. A belief in the right kind of diversity and the wrong kind of diversity. Workplace cultures where discussion is silenced and policies that seek to dictate what people believe, not how they behave.

In my work, I find increasing examples of senior leaders and teams failing to engage (*not my area*) or being scared to raise questions (*fear of getting it wrong – I'll be ostracised or worse if I say the wrong thing*) that has allowed an activist rather than a pragmatic voice to set the direction of travel. A much-cited example would be Stonewall Law v Equality Law (Cunningham, 2021.) Many cases involve positive discrimination masquerading as positive action alongside zero-tolerance policies applied without regard for context or opportunities for growth, posing real risks to organisations and individuals.

So, one of the key ingredients for success, if you want to achieve inclusion and progress equality, is to create a culture that welcomes diversity of thought and experience and values discussion. To do this, you need to lead by example. You need to test *solutions* and satisfy yourself that the course of action or policy aligns with the strategic aims of the organisation. This is conscious scrutiny in action. It requires confidence, even if that confidence is just to be able to say, "I'm not sure about this. Let's talk."

The third lesson is about cultivating confidence. Confidence in your own knowledge and being prepared and comfortable being challenged. Confidence that your team are making the right calls that will benefit individuals and do no harm.

Some of the questions you might ask yourself or others include –

» Do you know why inclusion is important in your organisation?
» Is this a shared understanding? What might we do to develop a shared understanding?

» If you/organisation X doesn't do work on EDI, what will happen?
» If you/organisation X does commit to embedding EDI in their work, what will be better?
» What do we mean by zero tolerance?
» As an organisation, do we have a growth mindset? Do we believe in continuous improvement? How does this relate to issues of equality, diversity, and inclusion?
» Can each of my colleagues say *that inclusion at my work is about me?*

A Policy Perspective
Policy, strategy, guidance.

Depending on where you work and what you do, policy will mean different things. It could be one or all of the above or something completely different. The fourth lesson is about policy development, decisions, and determining action – designing your destination.

In the context of this chapter, policy refers to the procedures we follow. It could entail recruitment policies outlining steps for advertising and hiring, guidelines for flexible work arrangements, or simply the norms for conducting tasks, like appropriate email timing. Or the policy might be the strategic aim of an organisation – *We are going to export widgets to widget buyers on each continent.*

Ultimately, policies are rules or objectives and can simply be described as *decisions*. Whilst the rules might be the same for everyone, there is a good chance the impact will vary considerably or that the delivery of an objective will need to flex to meet the needs of different audiences. One size does not fit all.

This is why it is necessary to consider the impact of the decisions you make. In the public sector, this is a process often called *Equality Impact Assessment*. I prefer to think about it in terms of Inclusive Design. I'll explain why below, but first a potted history of equality impact assessment.

Equality Impact Assessment has been a factor in decision-making for organisations subject to the requirements of the Public Sector Equality Duty across Great Britain and Northern Ireland. Similar frameworks are in place in Ireland and across Europe. The core principle is that if you are making a decision that affects people, you need to consider whether that decision will adversely affect people who share a protected characteristic or if the decision will perpetuate or alleviate an existing inequality.

The need for Equality Impact Assessment (EIA) first came into the consciousness as a result of the inquiry relating to the murder of Stephen Lawrence and the subsequent police investigation. The process of EIA was supposed to be a tool to tackle institutional racism, to move from being oblivious to the needs of people to making conscious decisions that required consideration of relevant evidence and the involvement of people likely to be affected by the decision. The need for EIA expanded over time to consider issues of race, sex, disability, and sexual orientation. By the time the Equality Act 2010 was enacted, most listed authorities had adopted an overarching equality and human rights impact assessment.

Done well, an EIA provides an opportunity to consider intersectionalities. Issues such as location (urban vs. rural), transport access, income, housing tenure, caring responsibilities, care experience, educational attainment, language, immigration, and refugee status can all be considered and *cut* by protected characteristics. The issue is that equality impact assessment is rarely done well, if done at all. It is usually a tick box exercise or a form to be completed after a decision has been made.

That's why I position this important work as *Inclusive Design* rather than impact assessment, putting the emphasis on building in inclusion rather than discovering the need for change when it seems like there is no time or resource to get on the optimal course.

When I am delivering inclusive design sessions, I reference cases such as McHattie v South Ayrshire Council (2019), an example of a cost-cutting decision that was made without properly involving those who would be affected by the decision. Or I may also give the example of a funding decision made by a non-departmental government body to develop hand sanitisers for the medical profession, only to discover that they didn't work for people who are melanin-rich. Anyone who has read Invisible Women by Caroline Craido Perez will have plenty of examples to draw on, from seat belts to PPE, which have not considered the needs of women. **The costs of failing to consider issues of inclusion cost money and can cost lives.**

In my view, decision-making is enhanced when inclusion issues are considered at the start of the decision-making process. However, in the real world, we rarely start from a clean slate, and the opportunities for systemic change come when the principles of inclusive design are applied to policy review. The challenge here is that the work on dismantling systemic barriers requires buy-in and commitment at every level of an organisation and very often requires challenging the status quo, often to the *perceived* detriment of those doing well in the current system.

This is a task made all the harder because when it comes to EDI, it is easier to collect the low-hanging fruit. Let me explain what I mean. As part of the Leading Kind Inclusion Audit work, I assess an organisation's starting point against a range of indicators.

First, I start by reviewing policy through an EDI lens, and then I engage with people at all levels and roles in an organisation, often customers and key external stakeholders. In addition to understanding what policy feels like in practice, I want to understand an organisation's attitude to compliance. I want to know if there is cohesion and purpose to the events that they run to *celebrate* diversity and promote equality and inclusion. I want to understand what they measure, why, and how, as well as the *so what*. And perhaps most importantly, I want to know what governance and accountability look like and how conscious the scrutiny is.

Courses and Compliance

Most organisations are now compliant by default. They have systems in place focused on negating the risk attached to direct discrimination. Policies are in place, and for the most part, people know what phrases and terms are racially offensive, and people are not (usually) overtly ableist, sexist, or racist in the workplace.

They publish information about the demography of their workforce, the gender pay gap report is published on time, and they will have reports, videos or similar that showcase what they have *done* to promote equality, diversity, and inclusion in the workplace.

Staff are *sheep-dipped* regularly and provided with learning opportunities about the nine protected characteristics and definitions of bullying and harassment and examples of indirect and direct discrimination.

The boxes are ticked, and the risk is mitigated. Or is it?

The reality, though, is that organisations (I am mostly talking about organisations subject to the requirements of equality legislation with a focus on the increased requirements often set for organisations delivering services to the public – health, housing, education, etc.) get their reports out on time, they very often take a lot of effort for little impact.

It wouldn't be unusual to read lengthy reports with pages detailing coffee mornings, training events, new lanyards, and screeds of tables setting out the numbers of staff who have or have not declared their protected characteristics, not to mention the acquisition of charter marks and memberships to illustrate the ongoing commitment to equality.

These reports will often have equality outcomes that state an aim to build an inclusive culture, increase the diversity of the workforce, ensure accessibility, and drive up data declaration rates. However, these outcomes are rarely SMART, rarely address persistent inequalities, and often duplicate actions that are part of business as usual. It is even harder to find the bi-annual update reports evidence of progress and impact. Again, this is usually reported in the number of things delivered rather than changes made.

At a compliant default level, we tend to find that the training covers the basics, provides chapter and verse on the legislation, and lists of *thou shalt nots,* but rarely provides applicable examples of how an inclusive approach can enhance someone's job or customer/ staff experience.

In this context, the low-hanging fruit would be the roll out of sheep dip training and acquisition of badges and charter marks without the focus on experience and change.

When an organisation is on its way to being inclusive authentically, we expect to see equality outcomes and key performance indicators that are grounded in research, address actual inequalities, and, most importantly, have resourced action plans. Further progress reporting is in place, and governance and scrutiny are in place to positively support the organisation in doing the work.

I would also caution against the pursuit of badges and charters as a means to an end. You can acquire a Stonewall Champion top placing but have a workplace where your gay and straight staff feel inhibited from expressing their beliefs or participating in LGBT staff networks. Or you can have a Race Equality Charter (many are available), but people may still be code-switching and experiencing racism in its different forms in the workplace. Furthermore, in the pursuit of equality for one group, it isn't unheard of to advise, protect, and champion the rights of one group in direct contravention of the principles of the Equality Act and employment legislation. Examples include evidence of *positive discrimination rather than positive action in recruitment in the armed forces and organisations being confused about what is and is not* a protected characteristic—confusion about sex and gender springs
208   to mind.

When organisations do not have training that is tailored to the roles and needs of the organisation, when the outcomes set are not really outcomes, this is an important time to think about the skills in place. Do you have people with the skills to commission and evaluate? Does the team charged with leading EDI have the skills to influence and manage change?

I think it is important to recognise that while it has its place in celebrating diversity, it is not enough to make people feel that their voice is heard and that they belong. That is why, after considering the position on compliance, I want to understand how people across an organisation are engaged in the efforts to promote EDI.

Diversity Days

Organisations use EDI to enhance their employer brand. No surprise, as research shows that potential recruits value an organisation's commitment to inclusion highly. Follow the accounts of well-known organisations on LinkedIn, X, Instagram, etc., and it won't take long before there will be a post about the lighting up of a building or new lanyards and notepads to celebrate a particular protected characteristic. The challenge, of course, is to make sure that the external promise reflects the internal reality, otherwise, the perception will be that the organisation is simply equality washing.

Key things I look out for when exploring an organisations approach to raising awareness of EDI are –

1. A lack of cohesion – I don't think there needs to be a centrally controlled approach to celebrating and promoting inclusion. In fact,

it is great when individual work areas want to shout about the great things they are doing or draw attention to an issue that is important to them. However, there is likely to be a greater impact when activity is co-ordinated and benefits from relevant expertise and insight across the organisation. Taking a beat and sense checking can prevent reputation-damaging missteps and can also engage more people from across the organisation in the conversation.

2. Exclusion – It is important that everyone in the workplace understands that their difference is valued. One way to alienate people is to exclude them from the conversation. I would always recommend that, as a starting point, an organisation celebrates the diversity it has and seeks to build on it so that everyone recognises the value of increasing this diversity. Knowing, of course, that our diversity is more than our protected characteristics. It is about our backgrounds, our interests, the things that frighten us and the things that give us joy.

3. Given the choice with a limited budget, I would always focus on embedding inclusion in decision-making as a priority, but as part of this, I recognise the need to build the burning platform for change. One aspect of this is the need to convey the message that inclusion is good for our individual and organisation's success. I would implore you to take an asset-based approach, focus on the positives, and make sure no group is excluded from

the conversation. It might seem easier and more visible to organise lots of celebrations of diversity, but getting that message over that you should invest in inclusion and make change happen is sometimes best done without the expense and resource drain of diversity days.

Management and Metrics

The fifth lesson focuses on what to measure, why you monitor, and how you manage for impact. I mentioned workforce demographics before, with many organisations seeking to improve the quality and quantity of the data they hold about their workforce. Frequently, I find the biggest data gap is not with employees in posts, but it is about who is and is not applying for posts.

To improve data quality for those people already working with you, you need to show the value of the information you are asking individuals to share. Use storytelling, for example, "We looked at our data and noticed that women of colour were not progressing proportionately, so we set up a mentoring scheme and board shadowing scheme. This has resulted in more people applying for and being successfully appointed to promoted positions."

You also need to show respect for the information shared and ensure people understand that their information is confidential and secure. People who may not be from the UK or Ireland may not be as comfortable sharing data for all sorts of cultural reasons. Ensure that data security and confidentiality messages are clear and consistent. Line managers and senior managers should not have access to identifiable data. As part of workforce planning, I would recommend that you engage with your pipeline data. What does the profile of university and school students look like? What should you expect your recruits to look like in 5/10 years? Is your organisation ready for these new recruits? Will you be the most attractive employer?

However, management and metrics go beyond the numbers of staff in post and outcomes at recruitment. You need to have a mechanism to take the temperature. Staff surveys may be one way, but I would suggest they are not the only way.

Other metrics you should be looking at include –

» Disciplinaries – Are people who share a protected characteristic more likely to be on the receiving end of disciplinary or performance improvement activity?

» Grievances – Are there any themes, particularly about types of harassment or bullying?

» Exit data – Are there any themes about location (teams) or protected characteristic data?

» Sickness absence – The impact of bullying and code-switching can manifest as stress and burnout, leading to increased sickness absence. Look at your sickness absence data to see if there are signs that cultural issues may damage people and drive costly sickness absence.

» Bullying and Harassment Reports – Do people engage, do they surface issues, or are they kept quiet? Are issues resolved at ground level, or are issues always escalated? Is the culture one where line managers are confident and capable, or not?

» Part-time progression – Does our flexible working commitment translate to career stagnation or enable career progression? Is access to flexible working more likely by people sharing particular characteristics?

Beyond metrics, listening exercises guided by trained, impartial facilitators are an important way to hear about the issues that are affecting people. Engagement with employee representatives such as Trade Unions and Employee Resource groups is another way. However, broader engagement, such as focus groups, is recommended to ensure you involve people who may not feel represented through formal channels. Combined, a thorough review of data and information gleaned from people will help you identify SMART equality outcomes and set priorities. This is about fostering confidence to focus resources on the most critical issue rather than merely signalling virtues without meaningful impact.

While demographic reports offer low-hanging fruit in metrics, the real impact comes from contextualising data, understanding its purpose, and devising plans to fill gaps for a complete picture.

Inclusion with Impact

The last lesson (for now) is about good governance, a culture of curiosity, and assurance that you have the right mix of DEI ingredients that make the right difference.

My research and experience all lead me to conclude that conscious scrutiny is the most effective way to set the culture and drive improvement. At the start of this chapter, I set out some questions about conscious scrutiny –

» At an individual level, how do you show your inclusion impact through the performance review or appraisal process? How is action on inclusion recognised?

» At a team level, how have we embedded inclusion in our activities that contribute to the strategic goals of the organisation?

» At a corporate level, have we progressed against the persistent inequalities or equality KPIs that we have set?

» At a governance level, do we understand the experience behind the numbers? Is no news good news or a concern?

I expand on these below:

» At an individual level, does every individual know what good inclusion looks like for them? Whether that's a member of staff in reception who is able to confidently meet the needs of anyone who might need their support or a line manager who is able to provide support and guidance to someone who is visibly different from them. Are mechanisms in place at appraisal or performance review to talk about skill development and the positive impact of their work against strategic equality objectives?

» At a team level, does your business plan have a clear line of sight to deliver strategic equality objectives? For example, what is it that your team does and how it accomplishes the dismantling of barriers to progression?

» At a team level, does your business plan have a clear line of sight for delivering strategic equality objectives? What changes are you making to tackle systemic barriers to inclusion?

» At a corporate level, do you have SMART equality outcomes in place? Are these informed by evidence and experience? Are you confident you are doing the right things, and do you have mechanisms in place to measure progress and listen to staff experience?

» At a governance level, is the board able to contribute to discussions about inclusion? Are the board papers metric heavy and experience light? Is the board able to add insight and expertise that is helpful to you? Do you paint a positive picture or an unvarnished version?

Effective approaches to appraisal are important, as are well-crafted job descriptions and knowledge frameworks that set out the expected application of skill and knowledge of EDI for different kinds of jobs at different levels.

Within the boardroom, diverse experiences are important for success. However, without effective secretariat support and direction that encourages input on complex issues and provides transparency about challenges faced or anticipated, the value of having a diverse and talented board won't be realised. A diverse board could become mere window dressing, fulfilling a checkbox for inclusion if it isn't properly positioned to address the most pressing EDI issues effectively.

I believe these six lessons will support you in taking tangible steps toward promoting impactful inclusion, aiding you in engaging with and grasping the vital drivers relevant to your team, stakeholders, and accountability partners.

Listening Lessons	Inclusion for impact
1. Build the baseline • Find out what you know. • Find out what you need to know.	*You know your starting point and your gaps and can use insight to make informed decisions.*
2. Frame the foundations • Establish the capacity and capability you need to help you deliver the change.	*You have accessed different areas of expertise – internal and external – to provide comfort that you are solving the right problems.*
3. Cultivating confidence • Take responsibility for your own learning. Start talking and listening to people. Avoid the echo chambers and be open to challenge.	*You are taking educated and informed decisions and balanced risks to make positive change. Listening to each other is just how things are done here.*
4. Designing the destination • You can only spend your money once, so evidence-based decisions that will give you the biggest bang for your buck. Doing fewer things well is better than spraying and praying.	*You are now undertaking inclusive design approaches as part of your decision-making and are able to make positive changes for everyone's benefit. You are dismantling systemic legacy for the benefit of those who have been excluded without detriment, perceived or real, to the beneficiaries of the traditional system.*

5. Measuring and monitoring

- Measure what counts, not just count what you can measure. Be prepared to change course if the insight indicates you need to.

You are compliant by default and able to show a return on inclusion. You have thoughtful measures about colleague experience.

6. Getting good governance

- Work with those who are responsible for accountability in your organisation to ensure inclusion is embedded and not an *add-on*. Be open to a new dialogue that could be challenging but ultimately impactful for your people, those you serve and those who hold you to account.
- Use your board. If you are not making the progress you need to, be open, let them know and get their insight.

Conscious scrutiny is embedded in strategy development and accounting for delivery. The right questions are being asked, and the right conversations are being held at the right levels.

CHAPTER 11: HOW CAN WE ADDRESS INCLUSION THROUGH AN INTERSECTIONAL LENS SO EVERYONE CAN THRIVE?

This chapter has been graciously contributed by Dr Liz Wilson of Include Inc.

When the penny dropped for me

"Hi, I'm Maya Rudolph. Do you love bad news?"

I don't love bad news, but I keep watching the video on my phone anyway.

Melinda Gates then says, "According to the World Economic Forum, it will take us 208 years to achieve gender equality in the United States."

Wait, what? 208 years? That is ridiculous, I think.

"Why is it that I can order a bag of dick-shaped gummy bears with same-day delivery, but I have to wait 208 years for gender equality?" exclaims Sarah Silverman.

Silverman makes a great point. You can even get Viagra on same-day delivery. There's even an app for it. I swear it's true! Google it.

"Women are currently less than 25% of Congress, and that's the highest it's ever been, which you know is fine because women are about 25% of the population. What's that? It's 50%?"

This one makes my blood start to boil. Our governments should represent us — both literally and literally. Literally in numbers and literally with our needs. But the video is still going, and I'm hooked. Note to self — stay focused.

"Here's a fun fact: in the Fortune 500, there are fewer female CEOs than male CEOs named James."

I laugh out loud, not because it's funny, but because it's absurd. Then Silverman perfectly sums up what I'm thinking before I am even able to articulate it myself.

"I gotta check my notes. Huh, that's weird. It just says, 'This is bullshit' on every page," Silverman says.

I imagine running up onto the film set of this video to high-five Sarah Silverman.

"Here's the good news: we can change this together," says Natasha Rothwell.

Natasha Rothwell gets a high five from me too! Actually, you know what? They can all have high fives. The video ends, and I look up from my phone and observe the people around me in the train carriage. It's a fairly even gender mix of people commuting to work for the day. Most, if not all of them, are engrossed in their devices, likely on social media, watching a Netflix series or playing Candy Crush. And more than likely, in this very moment, blissfully unaware of the gross injustice of inequality they will experience when they walk through the doors of their office building that day. I look a little closer at the women in this train carriage. There are definitely more women in their twenties than mature-aged women. There are women from a diverse range of ethnic backgrounds and probably religious beliefs, too, but I can't necessarily know this just by looking at them. Some have glasses, and some don't. I start to wonder if any of them are primary carers, are neurodiverse, have dyslexia or if any of them are living with an invisible disability like a chronic illness or mental illness. It becomes clear to me that while they all might be women, they are all so different. I then pull my laptop from my bag to start writing down my thoughts, and this is what I wrote on that day back in 2019.

"If the numbers are right and we are 208 years away from gender equality and we focus on creating gender equality alone, when will it be the turn for the other identities or groups of people? It would be thousands of years until we have equality for everyone. And to add to that, what are the chances of an individual being one label anyway? If we want to create equality and a world where everyone is included, we should be addressing the inclusion needs of all people and the whole person, not just one single group or one single facet of a person."

While I love the brutal honesty and mic drop

moments in Melinda Gates' (Gender) *Equality Can't Wait* video, to expedite equality for all people, we need inclusion to be about addressing the inclusion needs of everyone, not just women. It was at that moment on that busy train that I knew I needed to find the solution to addressing inclusion through an intersectional lens to drive equitable outcomes for everyone.

The Label Approach to Inclusion

The opinions on the reasons we are still miles away from inclusion are many and varied, depending on who you speak to. Take your pick from sociologists, anthropologists, economists, psychologists, political scientists, historians, or futurists. There are also plenty of academic papers and theoretical books that discuss the causes of inequality and discrimination. Discussing this would be another whole book in itself. So, instead, in this chapter, we are going to take a look at the common label approach to inclusion.

Firstly, let us clarify what I mean by the *label* approach to inclusion. This is the traditional way you hear organisations talk about addressing diversity. It's when we purely focus our efforts on the diversity identities independent of all the other identities, for example, the Women in Leadership program, the Pride project, the Black Excellence network, the Neurodiversity agenda, etc. While these are potentially important and valuable initiatives as part of the inclusion program of work, they are also a siloed approach to inclusion.

Honestly, I don't want to make anyone feel guilty

for pursuing inclusion in this manner. Experts, scholars, and the rest of us usually focus on the labels we personally experience as being most relevant (to us). It's human nature to start with what we know best, particularly when we are attempting to tackle something so big and pervasive. Unfortunately, however, this most often results in a blinkered perspective focusing on one or two of the big-name labels like gender or race. Yet the range of inequities that need addressing is considerably broader.

Additionally, organisations also have their favourite underrepresented groups that they focus on in their diversity and inclusion initiatives. These may have been selected because an issue was identified, for example, a sudden turnover of women in senior leadership roles. Alternatively, it may have been because new legislation was introduced that forced action, such as a disability accessibility bill, or a highly passionate, enthusiastic and vocal collection of employees that successfully got traction and support from their peers in the organisation, for example, an LGBTQI+ Pride group. When we focus on one or two labels, what about everyone else? Or what about the people who don't identify with that label at all?

The problem with this label approach to creating inclusion is that it is actually exclusive instead of inclusive because it leaves everyone else out. It's also an unmanageable workload if you decide it's important to create inclusion for everyone in your organisation. You would end up with so many streams of inclusion work for all the various labels, not to mention the combinations (or intersectionality) of those labels. Plus, it's missing the WIFFM (What's in It for Me?) because as soon as we start talking about one specific label, it becomes irrelevant to those who need to include others who are different from themselves. The label approach to inclusion is one of the core reasons we are still miles from achieving equity and equal outcomes for all people.

The Background to Developing an Intersectional Approach to Inclusion

There is a large body of theory and empirical evidence of the lived experience and impact of discrimination and exclusion on single identities, such as gender, race, ethnicity, LGBTQI+, and disability. Further, critical diversity studies have investigated the impact of intersecting identities, of which there are an incredibly large number of potential combinations of intersections. A few examples of intersectional studies include gender and race, race and LGBTQI+, and Indigenous and disability. While it is necessary to research and measure diversity and inclusion to understand the experience of people and the impact discrimination and the lack of inclusion have on them, there was a gap in the research and practice. Organisations and the individuals working within those organisations needed a solution and method to proactively address discrimination and the inequities and needs of all identities and possible intersectionalities.

Discrimination is a result of the decisions and actions of individuals, organisations, communities, and governments, which either intentionally or unintentionally have a harmful or differential effect on underrepresented identities. In this definition, identity is the aspects of a person that are applied to themselves, either by themselves or imposed upon by others. Identities may include but are not limited to gender, race, ethnicity, LGBTQI+, disability, age, and religion. Also, in this definition, underrepresented is not necessarily measured numerically. Rather, it refers to groups that, in context, lack power. For instance, women are not a numerical minority in society but are often underrepresented and experience discrimination.

While discrimination is commonly considered and addressed based on a singular identity of an individual (e.g. gender, race, disability), this overlooks the whole identity of an individual, which is constructed of multiple identities (e.g. a trans-female person of colour who has a disability). These multiple identities cannot be viewed or addressed independently of each other because they intersect to create one whole identity of the individual, which constructs a unique lived experience for that person. Adopting an intersectional approach, when seeking to understand the lived experience of diverse groups of people, recognises and values the magnification of oppression and discrimination when identities overlap. Intersectionality as a term was first coined in 1989 by Kimberlie Crenshaw in the context of inadequate legal frameworks to address the inequality and employment discrimination experienced by Black women in the United States (Crenshaw, 2014).

Intersectionality has now been adopted far beyond gender and race in considering the intersections between various other multiple identities and across multiple domains, such as in policy, law, advocacy, and organisations. In the United States, initially, public policy was predominantly critiqued through a feminist lens, coupled with black feminism, to highlight policy that favours and supports the needs and values of those in power at the expense of others. Race and ethnicity, class, sexuality, and disability later became perspectives to evaluate public policy for inclusion and equitable outcomes. While there is recognition that an intersectional approach to policy is needed, the complexity of applying the theoretical concept in practice means it remains a challenge for policymakers to implement.

Similarly, antidiscrimination law has struggled to apply intersectionality in practice, arguing that it cannot be easily organised or the cumulative impact measured. The laws in the United States protecting multiple categories of identity based on race, colour, religion, sex, national origin, disability, or age (EEOC, 2022) are a list of categories. When responding to identity-based discrimination, the law responds by focusing on one of those identities. Countries around the globe have similar lists of categories in their respective laws. This is further reinforced by the continued low success rate of intersectional claims brought before the court and the dominance of single-identity advocacy groups. While advocacy groups tend to share the same ideals as intersectional theorists in the desire to eliminate discrimination for all people, their advocacy work remains primarily siloed in identity categories, such as the National Association for the Advancement of Coloured

People, Global Fund for Women, International Lesbian, Gay, Bisexual, Trans and Intersex Association, The National Disability Rights Network, The Religious Freedom Institute, and The American Association of Retired Persons.

Researchers have also found limited evidence of organisations implementing an intersectional approach to tackle diversity and discrimination in the workplace. Furthermore, there is no consensus on how to incorporate the diverse lived experiences of intersecting identities into inclusion interventions. Instead, organisations are using a standardised approach that oversimplifies the complexities of injustice and oppression of identities beyond the single identities the organisation selects to focus their efforts on. Consequently, inclusion interventions invariably end up being identity-focused rather than addressing the inclusion barriers in the organisational system or the actions and behaviours of those who need to be more inclusive.

Now, please don't get me wrong. There is little question that those working on equitable public policy, in discrimination law, in advocacy groups, and those leading inclusion efforts in organisations and institutions are working hard toward the same end goal to eliminate discrimination and create equitable experiences for all people. While some progress toward equitable outcomes has been made, we are still 267 years from gender parity in economic participation and opportunity (Word Economic Forum, 2021), and we have been working towards gender inclusion even before the suffragettes took to the streets in protest for the right to vote over

110-years ago. Addressing discrimination one identity at a time, or in isolation, is not making the progress needed for all people of all identities fast enough. Intersectionality aims to challenge inequality, enact change to eliminate it, and provide a framework for analysing and interpreting the lived experience of the whole person and all people.

Consequently, many scholars have stated it is now imperative to put intersectionality into practice, moving from investigation to intervention. However, intersectionality's complexity and comprehensiveness are challenging for organisations and those working toward inclusion and implementing holistically and in a practical way. In response to this, researchers were specifically calling for a better way to apply intersectionality to address discrimination in practice and facilitate real change for the inclusion of all people. This is what led to the research and development of the *8-Inclusion Needs of All People* framework (Wilson, 2023b, 2023a).

Addressing the Inclusion Needs of All People

Organisations and individuals within them require practical solutions to proactively address the needs and inequalities experienced by all identities and potential intersectionalities. Efforts to reduce discrimination that fail to account for the complex intersectional lived experiences of people fail to consider and include the needs of the whole person and the needs of all people. The *8-Inclusion Needs of All People* framework (Chapter 9 Resources) presents eight recurring themes in pursuit of establishing a pragmatic operational framework for addressing the multifaceted needs of individuals across all actions and contexts.

The 8-Inclusion Needs of All People

» Access reflects the necessity to ensure all people can see and hear (or understand via alternatives) what is being communicated, and they can physically access or use what is being provided. This includes meeting the vision, hearing, and physical access needs of people, as well as access to property and facilities, resources, health care, credit, and justice.

» Space is about making sure people feel and are safe in the workplace and in the community they live. This includes providing a psychologically safe workplace that is free from bullying and harassment, where people can be their authentic selves and their physical safety is protected with safe work practices. It also means providing a safe space for people to meet their own personal needs, such as breastfeeding, taking time-out, praying, or administering medication.

» Opportunity requires that all people are provided opportunities to fulfil their potential through participation when applying for jobs and promotions and in education, training, and development.

» Representation is about ensuring all people can contribute, are equally heard and valued and can see themselves fairly and equally reflected in government and policymaking, the organisational hierarchy, pay scales, occupations, communications, the media, and decision-making.

» Allowances need to be made without judgment to accommodate the specific needs of people so they can do what needs to be done. This means providing allowances for people need to be the rule rather than the exception and can include accommodations such as (but not limited to) flexible working and job redesign, work scheduling and leave, learning and assessment adjustments, and work equipment.

» Language means choosing words or language that is suitable for the audience and does not reflect any exclusionary or discriminatory language. This means avoiding unnecessary complex language, jargon, acronyms, gendered or racial or ableist language, offensive or discriminatory terms and providing interpreters, translations or transcriptions when needed.

» Respect is the need to ensure the history, identity, beliefs, and values of all people are respectfully considered. This includes respecting the histories of exclusion and oppression and appreciating the impact that has on individuals and identity groups, respecting how people self-identify and how they choose to reflect and express their identity, respecting an individual's belief system and traditions and recognising and valuing the capability and contribution of all people.

» Support is about providing additional support to people so they can achieve desired outcomes and fulfil their potential. That support may include but is not limited to social services, policy and legal support, community and peer support, education and training support, support following a harassment claim, and organisational and leader support.

The *8-Inclusion Needs of All People* is a framework designed to complement advances made by intersectional researchers and to fill the demand for a practical and operational framework. Further, individuals, organisations and institutions can apply the framework to ensure that decisions and interventions meet the needs of all people and prevent discrimination. At its simplest, the framework can be applied as a set of questions or considerations in decision-making and designing inclusive solutions.

8-Inclusive Questions for Inclusive Decision Making

Using the *8-Inclusion Needs of All People* framework as a set of questions enables you to practice inclusion in everything you do, regardless of your role or function in an organisation.

» How will everyone see, hear, and physically

access without undue effort?

» How will the space allow all people to feel safe to do what they need to do?

» How will you ensure all people (including traditionally underrepresented people) are provided the opportunity to participate, be involved, and fulfil their potential?

» How are people with diverse lived experiences being represented and consulted with?

» What allowances and adjustments have been planned to accommodate the specific needs of all people?

» How will language or visual cues be applied to meet the specific needs of all people?

» How will you ensure the history, identity, and beliefs of all people are respectfully included?

» What additional support will you provide to enable people with diverse needs?

Using the *8-Inclusion Needs of All People* framework as a set of questions enables you to practice inclusion in everything you do, regardless of your role or function in an organisation.

To help get you thinking about when and where you can apply the *8-Inclusion Needs of All People* to your work, here are just a few examples of scenarios in which I have worked with clients to apply inclusive decision-making:

✓ Designing a new product so all potential customers can use it.

✓ Evaluating an existing policy so no one is discriminated against.

- ✓ Developing a process for a new way of working so inclusion is built into each step.
- ✓ Assessing the customer experience across the customer journey so all potential customers are considered.
- ✓ Selecting and procuring new tools, resources, or supplies so everyone can use them and your supply chain is diverse.
- ✓ Creating advertising, marketing, or communications so everyone is proportionately represented and everyone can understand.
- ✓ Establishing IT, privacy, or security requirements so everyone can easily comply.
- ✓ Determining the accounts payable cycle so small, diverse suppliers aren't adversely affected.
- ✓ Conducting recruitment so everyone has an equal opportunity to succeed.
- ✓ Hosting a meeting so everyone can fully participate.
- ✓ Delivering training so everyone can effectively learn.
- ✓ Starting a new project so the solution and outcome are inclusive of the needs of all people.

While the 8-questions may at first seem long and complicated to address, over time, they will become more unconscious and part of the process you apply to all your decisions and actions. Aside from facilitating inclusive thinking and potentially preventing rework because you missed addressing an important inclusion need, it's also certainly far more manageable than attempting to consider the inclusion needs of fifty-four different identities (yes, there really are that many) and the near-infinite number of possible combinations of those identities.

Recommendations For Application

In this chapter, I've consistently referred to *organisation*. To reiterate, the application of the *8-Inclusion Needs of All People* is relevant across various sectors, including government, policymaking, law, advocacy, and both private and publicly listed organisations, regardless of industry. To help illustrate, the following are examples of recommendations for impactful application of the *8-Inclusion Needs of All People*.

Government and policymakers can apply the *8-Inclusion Needs of All People* by:

✓ Extending the scope of people and needs protecting from discrimination without the need to list hundreds of identities and potential intersectionalities.

✓ Evaluating proposed legislation and its impact on creating inclusive and equitable outcomes for all people.

✓ Reviewing existing policies and legislation to identify barriers where needs may be unmet, overlooked, or unjustly oppressed.

✓ Consulting with the community and people with diverse lived experiences to guide discussion, input, and insights on inclusive solutions.

✓ Designing, planning, and funding community facilities, social services, and inclusion interventions to ensure they meet the needs of all people.

✓ Setting the local, state, and federal standards for inclusive practice and requiring compliance by government suppliers and contractors.

The legal profession can apply the *8-Inclusion Needs of All People* by:

✓ Moving away from establishing discrimination based on comparator groups and instead holistically addressing the contextual lived experience of the individual.

✓ Establishing an intersectional approach to evaluating and measuring the cumulative impact of discrimination experienced by people.

✓ Shifting the focus from identities to the sources of exclusions and disadvantages created by failure to meet the needs of people.

✓ Creating a framework for legal reform to protect the whole person and replace the existing separate laws protecting individual identities.

✓ Encouraging legal practitioners to broaden their knowledge and understanding of the needs of all people rather than specializing only in singular identity categories.

Advocacy groups can apply the *8-Inclusion Needs of All People* by:

✓ Breaking down silos and increasing collaborative efforts to achieve inclusion with a standard framework that works towards meeting the needs of all identities.

✓ Reducing assumptions or stereotyping of identities into singular groups.

✓ Validating the lives of people with diverse and unique intersectionality who do not see themselves represented in singular-focused advocacy groups.

✓ Reducing competition for focus and attention amongst the 'other' identities.

✓ Increasing a deeper understanding of the similarities between people with different identities leading to greater coalition.

✓ Speeding up the inclusion of all people as all identities will be addressed in inclusion.

✓ Interventions at the same time.

✓ Utilising funding in more cost-efficient and effective ways by focusing on inclusive solutions that address the needs of all people.

Organisations and institutions can apply the *8-Inclusion Needs of All People* by:

✓ Consolidating diversity and inclusion intervention efforts with a focus on common needs for all people and all identities.

✓ Providing a practical framework for people to use in their decision-making to ensure solutions meet the needs of all people.

✓ Aligning employee resource groups and efforts to a common goal.

✓ The review of existing policies and procedures is needed to identify barriers where needs may be unmet, overlooked, or unjustly oppressed.

✓ Evaluating and identifying inclusion gaps in the organisational climate and ways of working.

✓ The design and development of products and services to meet the needs of diverse customers.

✓ International geographies with disparate cultures and laws that may conflict with identity-specific inclusion.

As you continue to develop your inclusive leadership capability and lead others inclusively, the *8 – Inclusion Needs of All People* framework ensures you have a simple and practical way to ensure your decisions and actions address the inclusion needs of all people so everyone can thrive.

Inclusive Leadership Insight 40: Inclusive leadership goes beyond the concept of difference and is actually about everyone. However, we need to consider the needs of those who historically have not been considered in order to actually practice inclusion.

PART 5:
CONSTRUCTING
INCLUSIVE LEADERSHIP

Tools and Techniques for Change

We have worked to lay the foundations and engineer inclusive workplaces. Now, we are in the construction phase. This is the *how* phase. The phase which most people like to skip to, but without the first three phases, you will find this can lead to a lot of doubtful buildings with unintentional consequences. While this is in no way comprehensive, if the following elements are worked with, they can yield very effective results.

> *"Real change, enduring change, happens one step at a time."*
>
> — Ruth Bader Ginsburg

CHAPTER 12: WHAT TOOLS AND WORKSHEETS WILL HELP US LEAD INCLUSIVELY?

As the aeroplane doors swung open and I stepped into the sweltering heat of Bangalore, all of us were funnelling into the airport. It was my first trip to India, and I anticipated a transformative experience, which I got but not how I thought I would. I had envisioned a utopia, a serene and spiritually enriching environment where mistakes were non-existent and I could find a path to self-improvement. I imagined a journey that would lead me back to myself, offering clear answers and straightforward implementations. However, the reality was far more complex and untidy. The saying, "Everywhere you go, there you are," rang true.

Being inclusive and an effective leader requires us to have a relationship with self and with how we have become who we are. The following pages offer practices and approaches aimed at fostering inclusive leadership.

I encourage you to draw upon your individual experiences, insights, and challenges. These elements are critical as they bring context and a personal touch to your leadership style, enhancing your effectiveness.

These practices won't shield you from errors, conflicts, or power struggles. Nor will they create a perfect leader or perfect organisation. Instead, they are designed to provide you with the insight and ability to navigate these challenges more effectively. Just as my numerous visits to India seeking spiritual and personal improvement taught me, inclusive leadership is far from a utopian concept. It's messy. It demands continuous effort, active engagement to make a meaningful impact, and lots of critical thinking.

"Water finds its own level" my mum reminds me that what we normalise and how we interact with people become who we are and what we accept and expect. Inclusive Leadership practices are about co-creating our "own water level" together, rather than just accepting what is the default.

So, use these as a support, but know their effectiveness will directly relate to your engagement with them. No one else can do that for you.

Strengths-Based Approaches

So often, inclusion is seen as a corrective action that keeps us in the depths of what is wrong rather than what we can achieve. I truly believe in leveraging what people can do and aligning efforts with a strengths approach.

The positive impacts of utilising a strengths-based approach and adopting a growth mindset in various areas of life, including personal and professional development, are highlighted below. Positive psychology and a strengths-based approach can lead to beneficial psychological impacts such as boosted self-efficacy, resilience, and hope. Short-term strengths-based coaching can also increase well-being and optimal functioning for everyone regardless of their role within the organisation (Peláez et al., 2019).

Using a person's individual strengths can improve their performance. Individual strengths can be refined through practice and can lead to positive outcomes such as better work engagement, job satisfaction, well-being, and improved personal growth. People feel more valued and supported when their superiors acknowledge and nurture their individual strengths (van Woerkom & Kroon, 2020).

A growth mindset is linked to a healthier attitude toward learning, a better ability to receive feedback, greater resilience in dealing with setbacks and improved work performance over time. Using a growth mindset and strengths approach, individuals can boost their performance and achievements (Miglianico et al., 2020).

Coaching is most beneficial when the intent is to promote development. Additionally, hiring managers and staff who have a growth mindset can help reduce bias and prejudice. A growth mindset can improve a person's creativity, performance, and relationships (Han & Stieha, 2020).

Difficult People

While I can be the first to get stuck in the judgement that a person is difficult, I highly recommend we start to practice seeing our interactions with others as co-created. Rather than describing or thinking of a person as difficult, it can be really helpful to think of it as "someone I am finding difficult." This subtle shift is all about seeing the difficulty between us rather than within the other. When we hold the position that they are difficult, we can only get into a power struggle with them or reject them, rendering us less effective. However, if we see it as existing between us, we can ask ourselves:

» What am I finding difficult about the person?
» What in me is triggered?
» Realising I can't control or change another, what other choices do I have?
» Am I in my defence? (reacting, judging, rejecting, avoiding, people pleasing, arguing, stuck)
» How might my defences be making this situation more difficult for me?
» How might my expectations be impacting the experience I am having with the other?
» What expectations may be helpful to have, and what might be unhelpful in this situation?
» We always have more effective outcomes in situations where we are managing and processing our own dysregulation and emotional responses.

Control and Influence

So much time is wasted trying to control things we don't have the power to control. So little time is spent reflecting on what we can actually control, what we can influence, and what concerns us.

I am working with a number of organisations to develop inclusive leadership and organisational practices tailored to the organisation's needs that promote both effective ways of working and are people-centric.

These things help with employee attraction, retention, performance and effectiveness, and a sense of belonging, loyalty, and confidence.

Organisations that engage with some core change principles tend to get great results. While it is a complex process at times and often has unpredictable emergent needs and impacts, there are underlying principles at play that support creating desired results.

These organisations have figured something out. They need to do what is within their control, with the people who have control, in order to have an impact and stop wasting time. It is the same thing for individuals and teams. We often get caught up in trying to control the uncontrollable or complain about it, or get into power struggles and not focus on where our responsibilities, aka power, actually are.

We also tend to reject or try to control areas we only have influence over rather than engage with that reality. All of these things are power and time zaps and often distract from critical thinking and actual impact.

You see, one reason we do this and waste so much time on things that don't have an impact or utilise our power effectively is that it would have us taking responsibility and making changes rather than focusing on what others should do.

The underlying principle that has supported a number of leaders and organisations in having great results and creating a meaningful impact is this—focusing on the right things and people, to begin with and co-creating the desired results instead of trying to force them.

Putting it into practice.

Steven Covey speaks clearly about the circle of concern, control, and influence in his bestseller, *7 Habits of Highly Successful People*. I first came across this topic when I was training in Participatory Leadership in my home city of Cork.

I have found this most helpful when discussing people and situations. It has the most impact when someone needs clarity and to take effective action rather than anxiety-induced action. Covey simplifies the circle of concern, control, and influence so that it can be adapted easily for life and work.

Let's start with the circle of concern. This circle represents everything that worries you, bothers you, and plays on your mind.

Then, the circle of influence is the element of your concerns that you can influence by how you behave or what you say, but that is not directly within your control.

Some examples may be wanting family members to do something, trying to get a stakeholder to understand another point of view, or having your partner apply for that job.

You can impact each area by expressing your needs and preferences. However, you need others to cooperate with you to make any changes. Ultimately, they make their own choices, so really, all you can do is attempt to influence the situation. Whereas trying to control it could wear you out or build resentment.

Not to mention damage relationships and leave you disappointed.

The circle of control involves anything that you have power over, such as your choices, actions, approaches, and responses. How you do things is 100% in your control. How others do things is either in your circle of influence or not. You need to figure that out in each situation.

Start by writing all concerns in a big circle to the left of an A4 sheet.

Then, on the right side of the sheet, draw a big circle marked *circle of influence*. Inside that circle, draw another and call it *circle of control*. Decide where your concerns lie. Outside of your influence, within your influence, or within your control?

Place every concern into a category. Outside of the circles is no influence, inside the outer circle is the influence, and the middle circle is control.

Notice what is in your control and start by asking yourself, "How can I work with what is in my control more effectively?"

Look at what is in your circle of influence and decide how you will influence it without losing your energy trying to control it.

Lastly, look at what is outside your control and influence, and let it go.

Inclusion Employee Networks

The following is a set of general guidelines that may help you set up an *Employee Inclusion Network* (EIN). However, they are not rules. They are suggestions, ideas, and invitations based on successful employee groups that you can consider and mix and match according to the needs of your employee network and organisation.

I purposely call them inclusion networks and not *Employee Resource Groups* (ERGs) as I feel ERGs point to the power balance of the group being extractive, whereas an EIN points to the experience of inclusion being co-created and the network being something that spans across an organisation.

An employee inclusion network is different from an affinity group or other diversity groups within an organisation because inclusion is how the group works and what it strives to achieve. The group is focused on inclusion within the organisation, not just the group they represent, but the wider intersectionality of all people within the organisation.

Often, employee inclusion networks are used to ensure that groups traditionally marginalised in society can find useful and helpful ways to influence organisational decisions and support the inclusion of the traditionally marginalised group within the organisation. However, when the focus is inclusion as it directly relates to the organisational purpose, it is able to focus on why we need to be included and its relationship with the organisational purpose. Some groups that focus on diversity can see the role of the network in serving the marginalised groups' unmet needs in society first and then the organisation, which can be distracting from the organisational scope. As activism is high in relation to diversity and inclusion work, it can be easy for people attracted to these groups to come from a societal activist position rather than an organisational position.

There are many examples of the group's scope creep and then unhelpful tensions that are not progressing anything for anyone and may even be creating polarisation within organisations.

Employee Inclusion Networks are an excellent resource for creating an inclusive work environment. They allow you to have regular and focused conversations with people impacted by the group's purpose or with a particular interest or commitment to the group's purpose. They are voluntary groups in which any organisation member can be a participant. All voices and opinions within that network are equally valuable regardless of the organisational status of that person.

However, there is often some group agreement that those with lived experience and close to the topic are listened to with more care and sometimes more power, depending on the EIN agreements. This is so that their experiences are seen as valid and valuable input and not replicating marginalised patterns.

They can serve several functions, such as providing support and advice, speaking with like-minded people, peer-to-peer learning being used as a soundboard, a place to celebrate and engage in activities relevant to the topic at hand, and a place for influencing organisational decisions. They allow people with lived experiences and supporters to get involved and align with supporting organisational efforts and with sharing responsibility for inclusion.

Organisational Considerations

An employee inclusion network group needs to be integrated into the organisation's way of doing things. This may be a new way of organising within an organisation. For instance, organisations need to consider their culture and how aspects of their culture may limit the ability of the employee inclusion network to be a safe and effective space. So, before starting your employee inclusion network, it is important to say what parts of the culture may support us and what aspects of our culture may be limiting. This will allow you to set up an employee inclusion network that supports the purpose of the employee inclusion network rather than default to organisational norms.

Senior Leadership

It is helpful to have a link between the employee inclusion network and senior leaders, ideally informally, as it leads to more of a social connection than a tick-box process – whether it is that senior leaders regularly attend the employee networks to demonstrate that they value the content being discussed and so that they hear first-hand the discussions the employee inclusion network is having or, that different senior leaders attend different meetings rotating to ensure shared responsibility.

More formally, it could be a rotating representative to attend a senior leadership meeting to discuss the experience, focus, achievements, and requests of the employee network.

Power Structures

It is important to note that employee inclusion networks need to manage power dynamics within the organisation and society to ensure that the employee inclusion networks are impactful and supportive of their overall mission. It is essential to consider ways to disrupt power norms within an organisation, such as having chairs or facilitators rather than having set positions, rotating positions, or having formal roots in leadership teams, creating informal conversations with leadership team members. These allow the power structures formulated within organisations to work with rather than limit the process of an employee inclusion network.

Setting Up an Employee Inclusion Network in Your Organisation

First, consider how other employee groups have worked within your organisation and what you can adopt that will make this employee inclusion network easier to integrate into the organisation and, therefore, more straightforward for people to understand.

With the members of the group or at least with the founding members of the group, ensure that you clarify the overall mission and purpose of the group and ways of working. Also, there are ongoing ways of expanding the reach of the group and inviting additional people to join the group so that it does not become unconsciously closed or dominated.

Create a Learning Environment

One of the potential challenges faced by employee inclusion networks or any groups participating in inclusion activities is that an 'us versus them' mentality develops. Such groups may perceive themselves as being more advanced in their understanding than their colleagues or the organisation. However, it is crucial to remember that these employee inclusion networks also need to serve as spaces for continuous learning.

If members of an employee inclusion network fail to engage in a conducive learning environment and reflect on their own internalised prejudices or phobias, it could form a divisive mentality. This could lead to an unproductive 'better-than' approach, resulting in alienation and fostering an image of the employee resource group as being 'untouchable'.

While the role of an employee inclusion network is to provide a safe space for people to educate themselves and each other on matters of inclusivity, it is also essential that any misconceptions or internalised prejudices be addressed. This continuous learning and reflection process should be seen as an integral part of the workings of an employee resource group, not an instance of superiority or separation from other employees.

A culture of learning is fundamental in any inclusive organisation, and it is especially important that the employee inclusion network exemplifies this. This promotes the development of humility, cognitive complexity, and pro-diversity beliefs, serving as a role model for the rest of the organisation (Randel et al., 2018)

Group Dynamics

Influential and effective groups generally stay focused on the task at hand, so putting time into the group's purpose and mission allows the group to anchor itself when it becomes sidetracked or distracted by other topics.

A group agreement allows you to establish a shared understanding of how the group works together and performs, enabling us to create a culture within the network that is different from other settings. This is good for two reasons. One is that the employee inclusion network will function better. Secondly, it ensures that those involved in the employee inclusion network also practise what they try to achieve with others through role-modelling best practices within the employee inclusion network.

Relationship with Human Resources

The employee inclusion network requires a clear and established connection with the Human Resources (HR) department. The expectations HR has of the network need to be well defined. Equally important, however, is that the relationship is reciprocal and that HR is attentive to the needs and input of the employee inclusion network.

This two-way communication fosters greater understanding between employees and HR. It allows HR to better understand the experiences and insights shared by network members and enables the employee inclusion network to function more effectively within the organisational framework.

If HR wishes to engage with the employee inclusion network to help guide its own roles and responsibilities, this intention needs to be clearly communicated to the network. At the same time, a system needs to be in place that allows the employee inclusion network to express its challenges, concerns, or priorities back to HR from its unique point of view.

This reciprocal relationship will result in a sustainable and mutually beneficial experience for the employee inclusion network and the Human Resources department.

A formal way to arrange this is for HR to have meetings with the employee inclusion network or to attend, which can be helpful when there is an informal setting but a formal timeline for this engagement. This is also a chance for HR to see their steps regarding inclusion and changes.

Boundaries with Members

We need to be clear in what we expect and ask of people within the network. While we can ask for their input, we need to not outsource additional work that goes beyond their role to them, as this can result in unintended exploitation. We need also to be aware of who we ask to support this work. Otherwise, we could be perpetrating the very inequality we hope to change. If a piece of work is important in an organisation, then we will likely see people with varied identities engaging in the work and promoting it. If those traditionally facing workplace barriers are disproportionately engaged in these networks and supporting meaningful work compared to their demographic representation in the organisation, it could inadvertently add to their burdens and lead to burnout.

For example, if most of your inclusion sponsors are women in an organisation of 60/40 men, then we need to ensure efforts mimic the demographic. Obviously, in a women's network, you will have more members who are women, but in terms of formal sponsorship and senior investment, the purpose of the inclusion network shouldn't matter. The formal supporters should represent the demographic of the organisation.

Getting Started

Create a name that includes people who personally identify with the topic and those who value or support that community. Groups should not exclude people.

- Ensure that mission and purpose are organisationally focused and not societal, as that is outside the remit of the group.
- Ensure that senior people supporting it are not only those with a shared identity personal investment or who tend to be exploited by these groups.
- Build bridges between meetings and ensure members are connected to the employee inclusion network.
- Cross-collaboration is achieved by bringing different employee inclusion networks together to share what is working, what can be aligned across groups, and what focus we have next.

Inclusive Meeting Principles

These are a list of ideas that you can play with. They may be more or less relevant based on your context and what may be occurring in meetings that are resulting in a non-inclusive experience.

- ✓ Ensure that meeting engagements have clear expectations, and when possible, develop a group agreement.
- ✓ Ask people what they need in order to contribute well.

257

✓ Listen respectfully – Be wary of raising judgments and focus on what the person is saying rather than what you are going to say next.

✓ Only speak from your lived experience using 'I' statements. Avoid making assumptions.

✓ Principle of *move up/move back* – Consider the general flow of conversations. Don't force anything, and look to maintain a balance.

✓ Everything is adjustable – Trust your intuition and let yourself change things if they don't feel right. Speak up in groups and work together to meet everyone's needs.

✓ Balance your zones – Push yourself out of your comfort zone but be able to maintain accountability for yourself. Leave your comfort zone enough to grow but not enough to go into the panic zone.

✓ Confidentiality – If and when people confide in you, allow them to do so with the peace of mind that they can trust you. Never use anyone's vulnerability against them.

✓ Ask questions – Be mindful of intrusive questions, but if you have a question that needs to be answered to understand someone better, ask.

✓ Disagree with the idea, not the person – Be able to agree to disagree. Be respectful of others' opinions.

✓ Let people come as they are – Be open-minded and seek to gain a greater understanding of those around you.

✓ Be responsible for your own learning – Learning is an active, lifelong process. You are responsible for taking an active role in learning, taking what you learn here, and carrying it with you into all aspects of life (Simon Fraser University).

Measuring Inclusion and Inclusive Leadership in Organisations

Every organisation needs to make informed decisions, and measures can be very helpful. However, I also believe we prioritise what we measure, so choosing measures inevitably results in us deciding what is and isn't important. So, the measures we use need to reflect what is important, not what is easiest to measure.

Diversity metrics, in many ways, are easier because you are measuring something that is. In contrast, inclusion measurements are harder as you are measuring the frequency of an experience and the variables impacting that experience.

Diversity measures can include employee satisfaction or engagement surveys, feedback sessions, inclusion scorings, training and development participation, and promotion and retention rates. I believe these should fall under the lead responsibility of HR.

However, to measure inclusion, I prefer to stay closer to practices and look at efforts, successes, and failings. I see HR functions as setting up the mechanisms for success, but it is every single person's responsibility to engage in it. I recommend the following when it directly relates to what you are trying to promote:

- ✓ yearly surveys and questions
- ✓ 360 reviews
- ✓ in-built into promotional processes

✓ part of day-to-day assessments

✓ mimic previous strategies – such as health and safety or behavioural change approaches

✓ decision-making process linked to inclusion principles and how often we are using them

✓ require evidence of inclusive practices for hiring, promotions, KPIs and organisational benefits

✓ reward and value inclusion efforts

✓ measure intersectional identity and inclusion experiences

✓ inclusion meeting design and principles

✓ provide opportunities choices and tracking that

✓ measure the occurrence of change in an effort for inclusion

✓ inclusion employee of the month.

To quantify success for different measures, you could consider things such as data collection and analysis, defining baselines and targets, benchmarking against appropriate comparisons, regular transparent reporting, and continuous improvement (i.e. refine/adapt KPIs regularly).

Relational Repairing

"Love for Your Brother What You Love for Yourself."

———————————————— Hadith 13

An interesting thing I have found in this work is that we all want to be measured by our good intentions, but we equally measure others by their impact on us and not their good intentions.

Relational repair is a central skill for all leaders, and I would argue that it is for everyone. Relational repair is our ability to understand what occurred between us both and to find understanding instead of proof or rightness.

This is an ongoing practice I have to engage with as I have as strong an internal judge as anyone else. However, I truly believe that the work I have engaged in has had the biggest impact and has always required the skill of assuming positive intent and practising repair.

What does it look like? Listening to understand the experience of the other, avoiding the argument of what you did or didn't do, and focusing on the unmet needs that are presented in front of you.

It involves owning errors and moving through our internal self-criticism in doing so.

Workplace Boundaries on Inclusion Efforts

In workplaces, I really don't think we should force beliefs onto people. It is just not good practice. It is better to set up a set of values that you wish people to use in decision-making. This is not to say they need to share these values, which is the common misconception currently permeating organisations. Instead, it is to say that within this organisation, we want to see these values shaping our work. We collectively use these organisational values to influence our work.

Additionally, we also need to be very careful not to think that a change in mindset results in a change in behaviour. If this were the case, then we wouldn't have issues doing what we know is good for us. Instead, 261 we need to have clear boundaries around the desired behaviour here, how we want people to communicate, and how we want people to do their work. This means they can think what they want (to be honest, they do anyway, so I don't know why we pretend that an organisation can have hundreds of people thinking the same thing!) and what we need is an agreement on how they behave in the work setting.

How to apply this?

- ✓ Focus on what a good colleague at work looks like, which is different from the right beliefs.
- ✓ Make communication and behavioural expectations explicit at work.
- ✓ Ensure it is role-modelled, and when it isn't, it is addressed.

Leadership Identity and Effectiveness

One of the most pervasive misconceptions about leadership is the belief that a single approach will be universally effective. The notion suggests that adhering to a specific set of principles or behaviours will inherently boost one's effectiveness. However, the reality is far more complex. Most leadership literature, whether intentionally or not, is written with a male leader in mind, typically a white male. This phenomenon aligns with the "think manager, think male" concept, which has been extensively documented and discussed across various management and leadership theories by academics and scholars. My aim here is not to critique this phenomenon but to highlight that much of the leadership advice disseminated tends to be more applicable to white men. This observation is not to cast aspersions on white men but to acknowledge that the prevailing narrative around leadership and management often harks back to hero leadership models, which generally resonate more with white men than with individuals of other identities.

The crux of the matter lies in how individuals engage with their leadership development. The way you enact, perform, or develop new skills is intrinsically linked to your identity. This means that if your identity encompasses barriers or societal expectations different from those of a white male, you might find these skills and tools less effective. This disparity is not due to a lack of accuracy for some identities but rather a lack of universality across all identities. Leadership is not a one-size-fits-all endeavour. People first interact with you based on their perception of your positionality – your identity, gender, age, the language you speak, your religion, and how these aspects are presented. These factors significantly influence how you are perceived and engaged with in a professional setting.

What works for one leader, based on their identity, may not work for another. The effectiveness of certain skills can vary dramatically across different identities. Therefore, in your journey towards inclusive leadership, it's crucial to reflect on the barriers and opportunities unique to your identity. Consider how you can leverage your privileges to enhance your leadership effectiveness and open doors for others. Additionally, it's essential to recognise potential barriers and how they might affect your leadership. For example, if women exhibit confidence, they risk being perceived as arrogant due to the likability bias and societal expectations that they are nurturing and communal. Such perceptions can adversely impact their effectiveness as leaders.

So, when talking to yourself or advising others, acknowledge that identity impacts what is perceived as effective leadership.

Breaking the Phantasy: Overcoming Self-Criticism and Unrealistic Expectations in Leadership

Leadership is often associated with a phantasy that those in leadership positions or leading large companies or organisations are somehow superhuman and highly capable individuals. This phantasy can create challenges for people who find themselves in leadership roles, especially if they don't match the idealised image of a perfect leader.

All humans have insecurities, concerns, fears, and an inner critic, regardless of their leadership position. However, perceptions of leaders as being smarter, more capable, and having it all together can lead to feelings of inadequacy and self-doubt among those who aspire to be leaders or who are already in leadership roles. When we only see the external facade of leadership and leaders, it's easy to feel even less capable of the leadership role we're in.

This can increase the volume of our inner critic and raise our level of self-criticism. We may be overly harsh on ourselves, setting unrealistic expectations based on our perceptions and phantasies about other leaders. For example, in Michelle Obama's book, she mentions that sitting at the table with the most powerful people in the world made her realise that they were no different from anyone else. This reveals that leaders are just people who do their best, sometimes through power and privilege and sometimes through hard work, to attain their positions of leadership.

The reality is that everyone is just doing their best in leadership roles, and even the most powerful leaders make both good and bad decisions that impact others. However, leaders who are overly self-critical or have unrealistic expectations of themselves tend to struggle more in their roles. They may be overly anxious, stressed, and less open to learning and new information. They may also struggle with self-esteem challenges, constantly comparing themselves to idealised phantasies of leadership.

If you find yourself caught in this pattern of self-doubt and self-criticism as a leader, there are steps you can take to overcome it. One option is to seek leadership coaching, which can provide guidance and support in developing a more balanced view of your capacities and skills. Joining a leadership development book club or other communities of leaders can also help normalise the reality of leadership and provide opportunities for learning and growth.

It's also important to bring a reality check to the phantasies you may have about leadership and the qualities leaders should possess. Recognise that everyone has insecurities and challenges and that leadership is a complex and multifaceted role that requires continuous learning and growth. Setting realistic expectations for yourself as a leader can help you avoid being overly self-critical and stressed and allow you to be more open to new information and feedback.

Rather than thinking it's your job as the leader to create an inclusive, psychologically safe, and high-performing team or organisation, focus on how you can enable others to co-create that and share responsibility.

Remember that no one person can be responsible for everyone feeling a certain way, and we need to reposition it as a shared responsibility. Stop trying to get all the answers and start having conversations from where you are.

Manage expectations and see these as co-created. We all have a role.

In conclusion, the phantasy of leadership as an idealised image of superhuman capabilities can be detrimental to leaders by increasing self-criticism and unrealistic expectations. Overcoming this phantasy requires recognising the human aspects of leadership and setting realistic expectations for oneself. Seeking coaching, engaging in learning communities, and bringing a reality check to one's perceptions of leadership can all be helpful in overcoming self-doubt and becoming a more effective leader. Remember, leaders are just people who do their best, and it's okay to have imperfections and challenges along the way.

Inclusive Leadership Development Plan

Throughout our discussion on inclusive leadership navigating organisational complexity, we have intertwined the themes of inclusion, organisational performance, and inclusive leadership in a relevant manner. As we reach this juncture, it's crucial to contemplate several key points. Including where to begin, what to prioritise, areas requiring further development and what supports are currently available to access.

I strongly recommend revisiting the inclusive leadership self-assessment designed during my work with inclusive leaders at www.silewalsh.com/ilnoc

Undertaking this self-assessment again will enable you to gauge any shifts in your awareness and behaviour. You may discover that your scores have decreased, a phenomenon often observed as part of the learning competence model. This decrease is indicative of a deeper understanding of the subject matter, leading to higher expectations and insights of oneself. Additionally, you might notice behaviours you have become more consciously aware of, which you have started to adopt or engage with, influenced either by this book or the assessment itself.

In the realm of inclusive leadership, as with most leadership development, the goal is not to strive for perfection but to be the best leader possible within the current context.

I encourage you to reflect on the top three challenges you face in your leadership role – not inclusion challenges but everyday obstacles. What are these challenges? Consider their components and whether they also exist outside your work environment. Are they influenced by organisational life factors, such as market dynamics or social expectations? Identify the individuals affected by these issues and those responsible for addressing them.

Lastly, I urge you to revisit this book to evaluate how inclusive leadership practices can be applied to each of these primary challenges differently. Question who or what may be inadvertently excluded, overlooked components, conversations not occurring and thereby, innovative solutions not being considered.

This reflection, armed with targeted questions and a deep dive into the book's contents, will guide you in harnessing inclusive leadership practices to navigate and address the complexities of your organisational challenges effectively.

You will find the checklist at www.silewalsh.com/ ilnoc-resources

> *"Before enlightenment, chop wood, carry water. After enlightenment, chop wood, carry water."*
>
> — Zen Proverb

CONTRIBUTORS

Lynn Killick's career spans over three decades. She has navigated the complexities of human rights and equality, and built the foundations in a range of settings to support systemic change and enhanced inclusivity. As the founder of Leading Kind in 2020, she has turned visionary ideas into actionable strategies, making workplaces kinder and driving solutions that acknowledge systemic change's nuances. With a robust blend of practical experience and academic rigour her work is a testament to the power of evidence-based decision-making in transforming employment practices and building effective and inclusive workplaces.

E: Lynn@leadingkind.co.uk
W: https://www.leadingkind.co.uk/
L: https://www.linkedin.com/in/lynnkillick/

Dr Liz Wilson is a behavioural scientist, organizational transformation expert, and founder of Include Inc. Originally from Australia and now based in the United States, Dr Liz is well known for her authentic, honest, and pragmatic approach to everything she does. This includes her simple, yet powerful, Include Change Method that has achieved amazing results for her clients over the span of her 25+ year career. Dr Liz has transformed the ways of working and cultures of dozens of global organisations including: major airlines, banks, consumer goods, telecommunications, mining, rail, tech and medtech companies.

With a professional purpose that has always centred around the desire to equip individuals, teams, and organizations to thrive; Dr Liz's unrelenting curiosity also led her to research and find the solution to inclusion transformation, and reducing discrimination, with the development of the 8-Inclusion Needs of all People. She is now dedicated to creating a world where everyone is included.

E: drliz@theincludeinc.com
W: www.theincludeinc.com
L: https://www.linkedin.com/in/drlizwilson/

CONTACT

Sile Walsh loves supporting critical thinking, robust dialogue, and finding shared solutions in organisations that benefit service users and customers, employees, leadership and organisational life. Please contact Sile at Info@ silewalsh.com to discuss working together.

REFERENCES

A full list of references are available from
www.silewalsh.com/ilnoc-resources

IT TAKES A VILLAGE

Lynn Killick (https://www.leadingkind.co.uk) and **Dr Liz Wilson** (https://theincludeinc.com), your contributions are invaluable to our readers. I am so grateful for your work, ways of being, and commitment to inclusion. I am in awe of and deeply grateful for your ongoing efforts.

Tina, some people come into our lives and teach us something, while others come into our lives and help us learn. You have helped me to learn. Thank you for being my person and for taking this journey with me.

Mum and Dad, I would not be here without you, so I must credit you for that! Really, though, thank you for being my first role model for inclusion and compassion long before I knew either by title.

Mikey, Shan, Jake, Sean, Karen, Nathalie, Alisha, Luke, and Scott, I am lucky to have you in my life. Our relationships mean the world to me. I am always so impressed by the amazing people you are and how lucky I am to have you in my life.

Jo, you were the first person I ever looked up to, and you continue to role model critical thinking, kindness and authenticity all these years later. I am grateful for our relationship and for having you in my life.

The Walsh and Murray clans, I can't name you all individually because, firstly, there are too many of you, and secondly, someone might get offended. So instead I say this to all the aunts, uncles and their wives, husbands and partners who played a key role in my life, from giving me my first job, having heart-to-hearts with me, believing in me, backing me, for the handful who gave me money for sweets as a kid. For all the strength, you have role-modelled. For all the little moments, stories, support, and memories of kindness and care, you role-modelled for me. Thank you.

Jamie, thank you for always being there for a good debate and a meaningful conversation. You are one of my chosen family.

Thank you to all my clients and those who work with me in different ways. Thank you for your presence and the courage to show up and do the work. Your example inspires me to continue to do the same personally and professionally. Our conversations and reflections bring these topics to life even further than I could alone. Thank you for elevating my thinking and broadening my perspectives.

Calina Drakulic and **Francesca Lloyd**, you thought you would be filing papers and doing boring admin. You did remarkable work bringing this to life and making it inclusive with supporting resources. Thank you!

Myira Khan, thank you for everything. Our work is far from done; however, thank you for contributing to anti-oppressive practice in my work and, more broadly and for supporting me in my practice. (https://www.myirakhancounselling.co.uk/)

Dr Sebastian Green, while we are far from done, I

want to thank you deeply for everything and, more widely, for contributing to the work of systems thinking and psychodynamic approaches in coaching. It has deeply shaped my practice. (https://www.ochre.ie/)

Geraldine Walsh, I appreciate every word you tweaked, the conversation, and the effort you made. Because of our work together, I feel connected to and good about this book and its purpose. (https://geraldinewalsh.com/)

Thank you, **Gervase Bushe** and **Bob Marsh**, for holding the year-long seminar with us. It took me longer to publish the work that resulted from it, and this process informed some of these framings, as has all your work and my general approach to organisational development. (https://b-m-institute.com/)

Thank you, **Roffey Park Institute** and everyone who makes it Roffey; I have found that my work is more expansive because of the thought leadership Roffey nurtures and supports and the fantastic people I have met through Roffey. Thank you. (www.roffeypark.ac.uk)

There are people I haven't explicitly named, which isn't because of your impact on me or my work but because your influence was broader and in some ways less tangible. However as you continue to influence and support me and my work, I hope to find it easy to express the impact better.

Printed in Great Britain
by Amazon